HERE COMES

3

HERE COMES

THERE GOES

HERE COMES

THERE GOES

YOU KNOW WHO

HERE COMES

THERE GOES

YOU KNOW WHO

BY WILLIAM SAROYAN

Barricade Books Inc.
New York

Published by Barricade Books Inc.
150 Fifth Avenue
New York, NY 10011

Printed in the United States of America.

Library of Congress Cataloging-in-Publication Data

Saroyan, William, 1908–1981.
  Here comes, there goes, you know who / William Saroyan
  p. cm.
  ISBN 1-56980-030-8 (pbk.)
  1. Saroyan, William, 1908–1981—Biography. 2. Authors,
American—20th century—Biography. I. Title.
PS3537.A826Z468 1995
818'.5209—dc20   94-45637
[B]   CIP

First printing

Contents

1 The Witness 1
2 The Grapes 5
3 The Song 10
4 The Sun 13
5 The Money 18
6 The Snow 21
7 The Word 27
8 The Dance 34
9 The Reader 41
10 The Clown 51
11 The Fire 56
12 The Poem 61
13 The Ride 66
14 The Job 69
15 The Stones 72
16 The Thief 77
17 The School 84
18 The Nose 91
19 The Whistler 100
20 The Madman 106
21 The Wanderer 113
22 The Visit 116
23 The Eaters 119
24 The Millionaires ... 129
25 The Writer 133
26 The Gambler 141
27 The Bath 152
28 The Cat 158
29 The Fame 162
30 The Pose 167
31 The Winner 171
32 The Loser 175
33 The Automobile 181
34 The Foray 186
35 The Summerhouse .. 189
36 The Mourner 192
37 The Kite 194
38 The Debt 196
39 The Recognition ... 203
40 The Race 206
41 The Russians 215
42 The Playwright 219
43 The Letter 229
44 The Egg 234
45 The Papers 238
46 The Passport 242
47 The Place 248
48 The Time 253
49 The Person 260
50 The Purpose 265
51 The Water 267
52 The Rock 270

See back of book for an account of William Saroyan through photographs: a chronological review of his early years with the family, his travels, and some highlights of his career.

HERE COMES

THERE GOES

YOU KNOW WHO

1   The Witness

I am an estranged man, said the liar: estranged from myself, from my family, my fellow man, my country, my world, my time, and my culture. I am not estranged from God, although I am a disbeliever in everything about God excepting God indefinable, inaccessible, inside all and careless of all.

I am enormously wise and abysmally ignorant. I am also downright stupid.

My superficial manners stink and my profound manners are almost as bad.

I care so much about everything that I really care about nothing.

I try like the devil to be honest, only to have this very effort inform me every day that I fail.

When I try to decide why I am alive, or what is the purpose of my life, I am driven to either a frivolous and mocking conclusion, or to one of great earnestness not far from abject despair.

Thus, the purpose of my life is to put off dying as long as possible.

That's the frivolous conclusion.

There *is* no purpose, there can *be* no purpose to my life.

That's the earnest conclusion.

In between, there I go, never really knowing where
I am going, or why. I am little comfort to myself, although I am the only comfort I have, excepting perhaps
streets, clouds, the sun, the faces and voices of kids and
the aged, and similar accidents of beauty, innocence,
truth, and loneliness.

I consider nobody alive greater than myself, and I
know that I am nothing, sometimes arrogantly, sometimes decently, with a tender feeling for any form of
life near death.

I am sick of myself and have good reason to be. I
was born into this sickness, and I began to notice it
surely before I was three. There wasn't enough to me.
I needed more. Perhaps my fifty-two years as an ama-
teur human being have been a chasing after this
more. At any rate, I have always hurried. I have always
believed I hadn't very much time. I am astonished that
I have had as much as I have had. A lot of my friends
are dead. Sometimes I miss them and sometimes I envy
them. I have no enemies, but I know that this may only
mean that I have no friends. In a showdown, though, I
really wouldn't know who to hate, if I were to be expected to hate somebody, excepting myself. But I rather
love myself, possibly because I have never met anybody
else who has been even *half* as right as I am. All the
same, I still haven't a clear idea as to who I am. Am I a
mixture of Armenak Saroyan wed to Takoohi Saroyan?
If so, whoever he was, whoever she was, whoever they
were, he, she, they should have stood in bed, for all the
good of it.

I took to writing at an early age to escape from mean-
inglessness, uselessness, unimportance, insignificance,
poverty, enslavement, ill health, despair, madness, and
er of other unattractive, natural, and inevitable

things. I have managed to conceal my madness fairly effectively, and as far as I know it hasn't hurt anybody badly, for which I am grateful. I am deeply opposed to violence in all of its forms, and yet I myself am violent in spirit, in my quarrel with the unbeatable: myself, my daemon, God, the human race, the world, time, pain, disorder, disgrace, and death. I want what I want when I want it, and while it may seem to be something else, it is always actually the answer, the *one* answer I believe I must have and know, *now*—not tomorrow, when I know the answer must be a different one. Every day's evil is sufficient thereunto. I have made a fiasco of my life, but I have had the right material to work with.

It may happen that unwittingly I may make myself out a kind of hero in this work, but please don't be fooled. I am not yet clever enough to be able always not to fool myself, but don't let me fool you, too. I am the shambling man in the street you have passed a million times whose very appearance displeases you, as I passing you a million times have been displeased by *your* appearance, strangers though we were, and therefore obliged to be at least no more than indifferent to one another. You or your brother or your sister or your mother or your father or your son or your daughter were forever stopping directly in my path in the most stupid manner. And whenever anybody stood in your way, that was me. I am famous, it is true, but not the way you might imagine I mean. I am famous the way you are: as myself, to myself, and to the Witness, another word for God, most likely, and the one I prefer. If somebody, if something isn't watching us, what are all those open eyes everywhere? And each of us is certainly his own witness. The trouble is the damned play, human experience, which is diabolically tricky and most of the

time unacceptable. Hence, art, where I came in, and
where of course I go out, or hope to, although the odds
are against it, for no man has died as if it were a thought
he was thinking, after which he moved along to another
thought. I may not die a writer, I'm a cinch to die
Saroyan. I have thought about death all of my life, most
likely because my father died before I was three. I didn't
like that. As the years go by I continue to dislike it, even
though I am now fifteen years older than my father was
when he died. He died in San Jose, California, in 1911,
far from his birthplace, Bitlis, in Armenia. He was
thirty-seven years old.

Everybody is interested in everybody's last words. His
were, "Takoohi, don't beat the kids." I asked about his
last words when I was nine or ten, and my mother told
me what they were. I thought they were well chosen.
I thought he must have been a pretty good guy.

2   The Grapes

According to the story, I came about among weeds and broken glass, while the bell of a Southern Pacific freight locomotive tolled in the hot August night from just across H Street, in Fresno, California.

My father was on a vineyard in Sanger, twelve miles east, trying to gather the pieces together of a preacher without a pulpit and a poet without a reader.

My mother was hushed and angry in the unlighted ramshackle house, because now here was one more, making four, two daughters born in Bitlis, in 1899 and in 1902, a son born in Erzeroum in 1905, and now another son, in 1908, myself.

You've read this sort of thing before. So I was born. So what? Who wasn't? Who cares about that? Get along to the story. But then this *is* the story, this is always at least the *beginning* of it, and at the same time it is also always the one thing that is there all through the rest of it, because once you are born, that's it, you've got it, you've had it, you are the one you are, you are not anybody else just born.

I was the last of four, although nobody was sure there weren't to be any more, or that my father was less than three years from the end of putting on and taking off his shoes. And there was Fresno, a railroad town, nothing like Boston, New York, Charleston, New Orleans, Chicago, Denver, or San Francisco. A nothing

place, with eleven thousand people, streets A to U from
west to east, and from south to north with names like
San Benito, Santa Clara, Ventura, Mono, Mariposa, Cali-
veras, Divisadero, Tulare, and so on: Spanish, Mexican,
Indian. And there, all through the town, were the Armenians, from Bitlis, Van, Moush, Harpoot, Erzeroum,
Trabizone, and Diarbakir. Fresno meant Ash Tree in
Spanish, but I didn't find out until years later, and I
have never knowingly seen an ash tree. The meaning of
California was unknown, and how it came to be put
upon that enormous area of land on the Pacific coast
was also unknown. The year 1908 was the year after
1907 and the year before 1909. August 31st was the last
day of the 8th month of the year. It was all nothing and
nowhere, but I was there, I had just arrived, and there
was no telling what it meant.

My mother's mother, Lucy Garoghlanian, widow of
Minas Saroyan, was in the house, silent and not especially pleased about having given her daughter to a Presbyterian preacher who wrote poems. Every mother has
always got to believe her daughter might very well have
married a man of another order entirely. Who wants a
son-in-law who is forever astonished by the human race
and never able to understand a problem and solve it
immediately? Here was America, for instance, and there
was my father, but the man simply wasn't inventing
automobiles, buying and selling horses, telling lies,
cheating, or in any other way demonstrating a natural-
born ability to be a success. The kind of man Lucy
Garoghlanian, then less than forty, wanted for her
daughter Takoohi, then less than twenty-five, was a man
of wealth—that is, a crook from away back, with a nice
crooked father—and now it was too late, four kids too
late, two girls and two boys. For *what?* Poverty?

My father's mother, Hripsime, was not allowed in the house, most likely because she was the mother of this man who wasn't rich. She waited for word in her own nearby house, Hripsime der Hovanessian, widow of Petrus Saroyan.

Minas and Petrus, although both named Saroyan, were not related, Petrus having become a Saroyan by adoption. I don't know what his father's name had been, but it certainly hadn't been Saroyan, and so there it is at the outset, the problem of the name.

By rights my family name should be the name of the father of my paternal grandfather, Petrus. It doesn't really matter, though, because it would have been a name something like Saroyan: Krikorian, Avakian, Hovsepian, Muradian, and so on.

I was there, my father's name was Saroyan, and my mother's name was Saroyan.

My mother said: "Cosette, Zabel, Henry, and now what strange name is he going to give to this one?"

He came in from Sanger on a bicycle the following day and gave him the strange name of William, after his friend Dr. William Stonehill of New York, also a Presbyterian preacher, deceased three months. He wrote the name, place, and date in the family Bible, and years later I read it in English, and studied the same stuff written again in Armenian. So that was it, then, was it? William Saroyan and so on and so forth, may God love him or some such thing. And then he rode the bicycle back to Sanger, to the vineyard of his mother's sister's boys, the Muradian brothers, his cousins, where he was trying to get the hang of being a worker on a vineyard at harvest time. I suppose he was picking grapes, and I hope every now and then he was stopping to eat some.

The best thing about the whole place was the grapes:

the vineyards, the vines, the leaves, and the grapes. If anything means anything to me grapes do.

In London, in 1944, I used to pay a British pound for a bunch of grapes. I ate the grapes and remembered Fresno, my father long dead, my mother at last in a brand-new home of her own in San Francisco. In those days a British pound was worth about five dollars, and the only grapes to be had in London were from hothouses. I took Shaw a bunch of muscats and a bunch of ribiers, a yellow melon, and other fruit and vegetables, but Shaw was a real comic cut-up when he wanted to be, and he didn't get the idea of the basket of fruit and vegetables. He thought it was the occasion for another famous Shaw witticism, or whatever you might care to call a bright saying by an old man.

"Why does everybody in America think I need food? I have all I want. I can't possibly use any more. I'll have to give the stuff to the neighbors. I don't need it."
(Well, now, why don't you just settle down quietly and let the matter rest a moment, and after I get out of here, why don't you just pick up a bunch of muscats and just pluck one grape from the bunch and put it into your big loud mouth and eat it and not feel you have always got to be a great comic cut-up, because the fact is, you need grapes, you need them badly.)

"Well, I know you don't eat meat, so I brought stuff you *do* eat, that's all. No harm meant."

If he had to be a comic cut-up, so did I. I was the greatest comic cut-up in the history of Emerson School. What comparable reputation did he have?

I didn't mention, but not on purpose, that Takoohi Saroyan stood and held the edge of an open door at the time of the birth, so I'm mentioning it now, as it may be of interest to somebody. The midwife was an old woman called Ohskoh, a distant relative who enjoyed a great light-hearted reputation and knew her work well, knew women, knew kids getting themselves out, what to do, when to do it, how to do it, and not let it get to be anything like a big deal of any kind. She spoke softly all the time, not about what was happening, but about people, long since born and lately foolish. She gossiped, laughed softly, put her hands over the hands of the woman getting the child out of her, and soon it was all over, and there he was.

Outside, the weeds fought the heat, the broken glass cooled a little among the weeds, the locomotive bell tolled, and a hobo just off the train from San Francisco walked silently past the house.

My father didn't know what hit him. I'm going to say America hit him, even though I'm opposed to all such sayings. I'm going to say it, but I'm not sure I'm going to believe it.

"I'm a poet, a preacher, I speak and read and write English, I can take a pulpit and give an extemporaneous sermon that people can never forget, what am I doing picking grapes on a hot vineyard twelve miles east of a desolate town called Fresno? What in the world brought me to Fresno?"

Whatever it was, that's where I began—in the ramshackle house on H Street with the smell of the kerosene lamps mingling with the smell of flypaper.

Had I perhaps done it? Had I sent him nine thousand miles from Bitlis to H Street in Fresno?

Does the father decide, or does the son? Or does no one?

You Know Who

3   The Song

There was a lot of pushing going on before I came along, and immediately afterwards this pushing became so accelerated I couldn't resist it. All sorts of people and procedures were pushing me. Sometimes I hated it, sometimes I didn't care one way or the other, and sometimes I was glad about it.

And then I began to push. I pushed all over the place. It wasn't that I *wanted* to, I had no choice.

I was pushed, I pushed, I push, I am being pushed.

On the last day of August, 1960, the fifty-second anniversary of the day on which the pushing began, I found myself in Moscow.

A lot of people who are pushed don't even reach the following day, but I kept reaching the following day for fifty-two years. From the beginning the working of the engine was good, and I was there, complete with father and mother. I had their moles all over my arms.

All the same, this is not about me alone, as I expect to demonstrate. It *seems* to be, of course, but that's only because I am the one who is being pushed into writing it. At the same time this is not about you alone, either, if in fact it is about you at all, or about people alone, for I began to see birds almost immediately. And after birds I began to see other animals. One of the earliest was a cat which had an engine you could hear. There were dogs all over the place, too, speaking incessantly.

In Moscow I was at the home of a composer of music who sat at the piano and played a little piece he had just put together out of an old song of the Armenians. It was a good thing to hear, a mixture of sorrow and anger, and a push in the direction of love.

I listened to the piano and thought about the Armenians in relation, first, to the Russians, because Moscow is in Russia, and then in relation to the Americans, because I started in America. After I had considered the Armenians in relation to the Russians and the Americans, I began to consider them in relation to the English, in memory of Shakespeare, most likely, and then in relation to the French, because for more than a year I had been living in Paris, and had only lately gone up to Le Havre and taken a ship which had carried me to Leningrad. And then I considered the Armenians in relation to the Italians, the Germans, the Spanish, the Chinese, and the Japanese. I can't imagine why I didn't consider them in relation to the Jews and the Greeks. Perhaps it was because I think the Jews and the Greeks are almost as difficult to understand as the Armenians, but the following day I began to consider them in relation to the Jews and the Greeks, too.

Now, of course, the piano was going good, the piece of music the composer had wrought out of the old song of the Armenians was pushing out upon the music of other composers, other peoples, and it was necessary to marvel at how the man had managed this new thing which I could not forget for a moment was actually a very old thing. The Armenians in relation to the Russians and in relation to all of the others I have named were pretty much the same as the Armenians *not* in rela-

ie Russians or anybody else, excepting perhaps
:nians in relation to the Armenians, and then
you had to know which Armenian in relation to which
other Armenian, and the music was too interesting to
permit any such speculation. All right, one Armenian
might very well be the traditional rug merchant of the
jokes of America and the other might be the poet, or
my father. The rug merchant sold a rug, and my father
wrote a poem. In the poem my father said he was far
from the place of his birth, and then he said he was
far from his purpose, and finally he confessed he was far
from everything. In short, a lyric poem. The rug merchant received money for his rug, my father received
nothing for his poem.

The minute the composer stopped playing I said,
"Play it again."

Now, at that time there were thirty-three of us in the
study of the composer, and for some reason everybody
was confused by my request. The composer, on the other
hand, immediately began to play the whole thing over
again, and this time, if anything, played it better than
the first time, and there I was, fifty-two years old right
down to the last minute.

After the party, on my way to the hotel where I was
stopping, I noticed that the time was half past two in
the morning. I walked through Red Square and across
the bridge, because I had taken the same walk in 1935
when I had been twenty-seven years old. I like walking
across a bridge and looking down at a river. I walked
until daybreak and tried to think why I had been
crying lately.

4   The Sun

The head-shrinker will smile and think he knows why, and he may not be mistaken, either, but only I know the real reasons. There are a lot of them, and some of them contradict others. I have come to tears because love of truth has made a liar out of me. It doesn't help matters any that I am an unwilling liar, or that others are worse liars than I am. And by others I mean only men of art, science, religion, and life. I put life in that group, because I believe there are a number of lucky people in the world who manage their involvement with time, matter and energy, in a way that makes the mere fact of being alive an achievement comparable to the writing of a great poem, and possibly surpassing it in importance.

But I reject all this, all that I have just said, all that I have implied, and all that I have left unsaid.

I reject all that I know, even while I am taking up for examination something *new* that I know, or believe I know. I reject meaning itself, because it just doesn't mean anything. It means all sorts of things of course, some of them quite impressive, but immediately after the recognition of this meaning, even *during* this recognition, I also know the meaning is meaningless, and useless.

Who do we think we are and what do we think we're doing?

At the same time I have been laughing lately. There has always been a lot to laugh about, by which I mean all of it has always been misunderstood. I have always been able to believe that eventually enough time would have passed through my being, awake and asleep, to permit me neither to laugh nor cry, but here I am, perhaps the oldest young man in the world, and still enough time has not passed through me for *that*.

We are all liars because we exist, survive, and communicate by means of words, and words lie. Actually, everything lies: words, numbers, signs, gestures, facial expressions, animal sounds, songs, dances, everything we have.

The best thing we have is sleep, of course, and what is sleep except the putting aside of everything tentative for another interval of final and everlasting truth? Sleep isn't dying, but it is certainly keeping in touch with it.

Awake, nothing is true, nothing makes sense for me, although I have always believed the arrival of an enormous sum of money into my life would make a little sense. It didn't, though. The money arrived, and everything was *still* senseless. We need the sun, and I especially need it, but it has been years since I have given the sun even a moment of thought. I used to think about the sun all the time, all day long and far into the night. I used to wake up in the middle of the night and think about it. I can't imagine why I stopped thinking about it. I used to think about its size and what it is composed of, and what it does. I love death, I have always loved it, I have always hated it, but there is something between death and myself that is very close, closer than anything else I have with anything else, but I hate the idea of losing the sun. I want to go along with death, but I don't want to leave the sun. If I had my life to live over again, I would live it over again, never knowing I was living it over again, just as it has been so far *this* time. The fellow who came along with his screwball talk surely meant to help, but he didn't at all, did he? And if he had been a writer of plays, as I am, as I have been, as I shall go on being, wouldn't he have had a great time with the critics? Wouldn't they have expected him to lay off the double-talk and tell them in plain language what he was driving at? God's only son indeed. Who *wasn't*?

Well, of course, he was giving a performance, and *that* was his part.

I am addicted to the giving of a performance, too, and *my* part is the natural writer. I have difficulty knowing for sure if anything I do is not a performance. Some performances are good, or I think they are, and some are bad, or I think they are, but I am always compelled to suspect that in either event I am mistaken. But the fact remains that I am a writer, and I've got to write.

Nobody *asked* me to write. Nobody asked me anything. I was there, and I didn't know any better. I picked and I chose, and it came to writing, so here I am in this fifth-floor flat in Paris, which is now my home. Here I am still writing. If you don't say it in three million words, you aren't likely to say it, are you? Well, I've used up a great many more than three million words, and I still haven't said it. And the reason for that may very well be that it isn't to be said. We write and we read, and it makes a pleasant diversion, but it doesn't mean very much, and it doesn't help. Of course everything helps a little, but not really. The brilliant thing is not to care that it doesn't, and most of the time we

are pretty good at that. If we weren't, we would have
destroyed ourselves long ago. Every man destroys himself sooner or later by means of things said to be good
or by means of things said to be bad. Good or bad, it
comes to the same thing. The man killed himself. It
took him twenty years or it took him eighty, but he did
it, he finally made it. There is no man who has not
found being alive contemptible. Being a human being
just doesn't figure, that's all. But there is always work
to do, there is always time to kill, and a man does his
work and kills his time. I chose writing because it keeps,
and very little else does.

Sherwood Anderson, for instance, killed himself by
swallowing a toothpick, which punctured him somewhere, causing peritonitis, the same condition that killed
my father, who got his peritonitis from a ruptured ap-
pendix. Sherwood's toothpick came with an olive at-
tached to it in a martini at a cocktail party. No man
should have an accident like that and then pay for it
with his life, but long before the accident, Sherwood
Anderson had gotten fat, and that was probably the real
accident that caused his death, or the accident by means
of which he killed himself. I saw him fat when I was
lean and hungry. I felt ashamed for him, because I
couldn't understand what he was doing standing in
front of a room full of middle-aged clubwomen, talking.

"I'll never get fat," I thought. "I'll never do that.
Stand there like a blithering idiot."

But I *got* fat. I *am* fat. And all that remains now
is for me to stand there and talk to the ladies.

I chose writing because I get bored quickly, and I
imagined that there would be a million ways to write
and a million things to write about, and so I wouldn't
be so likely to be bored as I might otherwise be. I

was entirely unmistaken in this. There *are* a million things and a million ways to write about them, but if it is yourself doing the writing, it is *always* yourself, and while you are never entirely the same from day to day, enough of you *is* the same to make it almost as boring as doing anything else, or doing nothing at all. Still, it *is* a good way to go.

I don't expect to *see* the sun when I'm dead, but will I *remember* it, even?

5   The Money

Now, when I look over the debris of my life, I am dumb-
founded, flabbergasted, astonished, bewildered, dis-
gusted, and filled with shame and regret. What did I do
wrong? Where did all of this junk come from? There on
the floor beside my desk are the eleven wrappers in
which I had carefully folded great numbers of traveler's
checks, which I had expected to use thoughtfully, intel-
ligently, meaningfully, only to have thrown the money
away at gambling. And there's the lie again. I didn't
throw the money away at all. I went in there and put
the money on the line because I meant to win, because
I believed I *would* win, because I needed to win, because in all the world, in all the range of human experience, I believed nothing was more right, more appropriate, more desirable, more exalted than to go on in
there and gamble, to bet I would be right and not
wrong. And of course I *was* right, but still I lost. Must
I therefore believe I went in there to kill myself? Did
I go in there *not* to win at all, still believing nothing
was more right than to go in there and put my money
on the line? I want to tell the truth, but I don't know
the truth, and I am annoyed about not knowing it and
not being able to arrive at it. If I agree to something,
            hat's all, but that doesn't make what I have

agreed to the truth, it only makes it an agreement. I went in there to drink and get some quick answers about the great raw product called money, by which all things thrive and perish. I went in to raise hell with hell, and I raised hell. I liked it, I enjoyed every minute of it. I guess I might say I was somebody else at the time, but it was certainly my own name I signed at the bottom of the traveler's checks, so it must have been me.

It was certainly my own money I was peeling off and throwing around, the money with which I meant to buy a vineyard in the south of France or the north of Spain, but there I was, glad to be there, drunk, a loser, and howling like a dervish with the joy of truth, in a stupid mansion of a gambling house in Nice. Nothing was any good in Nice except when I was in the gambling house again, drinking again, because I was sure, I was positive, this was the way to live, this was the way to make sense, win or lose, this was truth, and now, a little more than a year later, there on the floor are the empty black plastic folders, one after another. The money's all gone, and I'm angry, because other playwrights keep their money.

And I'm jealous, because every actor I ever met got more girls than I did.

Imagine, if you will, being jealous of an actor. Could anything be more disgusting?

In a newspaper or in a popular magazine I see an actor, dangling somewhat as if from a string held by a hidden puppeteer, and beside him I see a magnificent Italian girl who is all mouth, mama, and murder, and I get jealous all over again. That's the girl *I've* been looking for, how come the actor gets her? What does he *talk* to her about? And he gets so many of the girls, one after another, six or seven in a row, and as many as a

dozen going at once, all over the world. That makes me
jealous. I've heard he can act, but who *can't* act? Who
doesn't? What's all this acting stuff about? I can act, too.
I've been acting all my life, but not for any little audience you can find in a movie. I act for acting's own
ridiculous sake, for no reason at all, for anybody and
everybody, but most of all for the One, the Witness,
and not in any little story like the stories movies are
made out of, or any little play some hungry or overfed
playwright has managed to write, either. I act all over
the place, but I don't get the girls the actor gets. Is his
secret knowing how to be nice to them, knowing all the
while that he's lying, he really doesn't care for any of
them, he just doesn't know where else to go in his spare
time? Then, why did he say in the magazine interview
he wanted to go to India? Why did he say *that?* If he
doesn't know where else to go in his spare time, why did
he say he wanted to go to India? I went to India and I
didn't even want to go. I walked in Bombay and I saw
nothing but hot little men and women who *really* didn't
know where to go. The actor and I, we will both be gone
soon enough, and I am jealous because he will have had
all those girls and I will not have had them. It burns me
up.

6   The Snow

In 1928 I was obliged to go from San Francisco to New
York, a distance of three thousand miles, although whenever I have had occasion to speak of the distance in one
or another of my stories or plays I have said the distance is *three thousand three hundred and thirty-three
miles,* because I like numbers to be interesting and to
have identities, the same as people. Three thousand
hasn't got that little extra something that is the difference between a great piano player like Richter, for instance, and a poor piano player like my cousin Hoosik,
for instance, who is actually a lawyer. Three thousand
both sounds and looks monotonous, whereas the journey
itself isn't monotonous at all. And how should any man
know for sure precisely how far he has traveled in going
from San Francisco to New York? In short, the whole
thing could very well be gossip, and if we're going to
gossip, I would prefer to pick and choose my own style.

When I say I was obliged to go from San Francisco
to New York, you may imagine that I was sent on an
errand of some importance. No such thing. I didn't even
have the bus fare, which was $38 in those days,
but my father's younger brother Mihran loaned me the
money. As a matter of fact he loaned me $200, although
the bus company made a mistake and shipped my suitcase to New Orleans instead of to New York, and all of

my money was sewn inside my sweater by my grandmother Lucy.

The bus bounced into a ditch in Kansas and fell on
its side, and somewhere else it ran over a pig, and somewhere else it was struck by a man pushing a wheelbar-
row with a load of bricks in it, and each of these events
took time. Everybody got out of the bus and met everybody who came to see what had happened. They ex-
changed names and addresses as if they were the first to
do something spectacular, and everybody was courteous
and sincere, as all great people are. I kept telling the
driver, "Come on, Max, let's get to New York, shall we?"
But he claimed we'd be there soon enough, don't worry
about that. I'd soon understand what a fool I had been
to leave home and hearth and meals cooked by my
mother.

At last the bus reached New York. It stopped at the
bus station near the old Waldorf Astoria Hotel on
34th Street and Fifth Avenue which was torn down
a few years later to make room for the Empire State
Building. By going up high that way, you reached free
space. You could see for yourself, though, that no matter how high you went, there was still a lot of room up
there. I was always satisfied only to *look* up. I never
really envied the birds and did not feel I had been left
out of things when I was denied the ability to flap my
arms and fly into the sky. I enjoyed having my feet on
the earth, or rather on the sidewalk, because once I was
in New York it was all sidewalk.

A few days after I arrived I was twenty years old. I
felt deceived and discouraged, or at any rate short of
money, as my suitcase was still lost. I didn't find out that
it had been shipped to New Orleans by mistake until a
couple of weeks later, by which time I knew more about

New York than a great many people who were born there. I knew most of the free places, especially the Public Library on Fifth Avenue and 42nd Street, which was practically my home away from home.

My second day in New York I found a job with the Postal Telegraph Company which was later bought out by the Western Union Telegraph Company. At six every morning I opened a small branch office on Warren Street in the wholesale produce district, and so I was free every afternoon at three, whereupon I took off for what might be said to have been the New York adventure. I traveled by foot, by subway, by elevated, by bus, by streetcar (later they took out the streetcar lines, and still later they got rid of the elevated lines, too).

Why did I go to New York?

I went there because I was an immigrant, and all immigrants go to New York. My father went to New York, why shouldn't I go to New York? And I went there to see about improving my style. The bus ride gave me a pretty good idea about the size of the country, and New York gave me a pretty good idea about the size of a big city, and the way people live in a big city. They lived the same way people in Fresno lived, except that in November it began to snow.

I said to a messenger named Peter Beaufrere, "Pete, there's style for you, there's real style for you, that snow falling is the finest style I've ever seen, and if I could ever learn to write the way that snow is falling my fame and fortune would be made."

Peter Beaufrere whispered, "Don't let anybody hear you talking that way or they'll take you to Central Islip."

Peter Beaufrere had spent a year and a half at Central Islip because a number of foolish people had certified him. Pete believed I was mad, too, but he didn't want me to be taken to Central Islip, so he was always whispering suggestions about how I could avoid going there. I enjoyed talking to him because he didn't feel it was absurd for me to believe I was a writer. He just felt I ought to avoid being certified.

Every morning when he arrived at the office he would smile and say, "We're all right, aren't we? We're *both* all right, aren't we? Let them say anything they like, we're all right, we're just as all right as they are, they can't take us to Central Islip, can they?"

We were good friends. I wanted to write and Pete wanted to stay out of the lunatic asylum.

Every evening after I had gotten tired of exploring New York I went to the Public Library, ordered six or seven carefully selected books, sat down at a table and began to read around in them. If all of the writers of the books in the Public Library had found out how to write, I ought to be able to find out, too.

With my first wages I bought a portable typewriter and wrote an essay called *The Mentality of Apes,* which was about me, or rather about Peter Beaufrere and me. But if you want the whole truth it was about all of the people in New York, because they seemed to be only an inch and two-thirds removed from the ape. It was an amusing piece, I thought, but I'll never know for sure because the magazine I sent it to, called *The Brooklynite,* never sent it back. And there's another great work by an unknown young writer lost forever.

Now, when you're twenty, when you're three thousand three hundred and thirty-three miles from home, when you're a writer who hasn't made his fame and fortune, when it's snowing all the time and six million people are knocking themselves out trying to get through the slush on the sidewalk to a cup of coffee, you stop to think. You think, "At this rate I'll never make my fame and fortune. I'm twenty years old. I've been in New York three and a half months and I *still* haven't written a famous book. In less than two weeks it will be 1929, and what good will that do me, still unknown?"

I stopped to think every ten or fifteen minutes, but the thinking didn't do me any good, so I decided to forget thinking, forget writing, forget fame and fortune. That night I forgot to turn off the gas-jet in my new room on 43rd Street just off Broadway. That is to say, I turned it off, but not in the proper manner, from never having operated a gas-jet before. I put out the flame but turned on the gas again, and went to sleep. When I woke up something smelled funny. All of the air in the room smelled gassy. I thought I had better have a cigarette, and then I thought I'd better not. I went out into the hall to see about finding the landlady, so she could show me how the thing worked. She shut off the gas and I got dressed and went to the office on Warren Street and slept on the counter. At six when Peter Beaufrere reached the office I was still asleep on the counter.

He rapped on the window, and when I opened the door he said, "If anybody asks me if you slept on the counter I'll tell them they're crazy." He was whispering and looking around for anybody who might be listening. "Just because you slept on the counter doesn't mean you're crazy, but if anybody asks if you slept on the counter, we'll *both* tell them you slept at home in your bed. What did you sleep on the counter for?"

I told him about the gas-jet. Wouldn't you know I'd rent a room in New York in 1928, and it would have to be one of the last rooms in the whole city that was lighted by gas instead of electricity?

"Don't tell anybody," Pete whispered. "It's all right to tell me. I won't tell anybody. They'll never take *us* to Central Islip, will they?"

Well, of course they didn't. Pete and I fought through to an acceptable appearance of ordinariness. It was a great time. There were some great people in New York in 1928. I was one of them, Peter Beaufrere was another, and then each of the other six million people, one by one. It was just a question of meeting them and finding out for yourself.

I never did learn the secret of the style of the snow, though.

I wrote working-class Armenian writing in English. It was always bad writing, but I was stubborn, and finally the editors threw up their hands in despair and started to print the stuff anyhow.

7   The Word

It may be, however, that you expect to be *inspired* by what you read. Why not?

You *are* all right.

You *can* find out how to bring up out of the depths of your being an ancient wisdom and put it to work in the making of money.

If you want to be welcome wherever you go, if you want people to smile when they see you, if you want them to marvel at everything you say, you can learn how to be that kind of man, woman, or child instead of the unfortunate man, woman, or child you have needlessly been for so long. If you want to move up in the world and meet the leaders and answer their troubled questions about what we are to do with ourselves, you can do that, too. The leaders weren't always up that way, they had to *move* up, too. They had to fight and push and shout and trip and knife and strike to get where they are, and of course you can do these things, too.

Or if you have a weight problem, you can take off all the weight you like, and still eat three wholesome nourishing meals a day, without perhaps only that extra thin slice of zwieback, that's all. I am here to help as much as I possibly can, and I am not asking you to help me because there is no help for me. I had my chance and I let it go. I might very well be on the front pages

of every newspaper in the world tomorrow morning if
I hadn't at the age of nine decided against it. But that
doesn't mean you have got to decide against leading,
too. You absolutely do not have to be a natural-born
leader to lead. You can work up to it, and from the deep
inner collective sources of your soul bring forward the
great strength and wisdom that is the mark of the rat,
the righteousness of ratness, as against the unrighteous-
ness of mouseness. Learn how to bring down the opposi-
tion, to destroy the quiet man with the intelligent mind,
to answer the stupid question of the fool who would like
to know precisely *why* you are leading. Tell him it is for
humanity, and learn how to believe your answer *is* the
truth. It isn't easy to do, but with a little practice you
can learn to do it. Other leaders have left perfectly clear
instructions on how this can be achieved, and of course
I'm giving you the hang of it in capsule form. It's
for humanity. Always remember that. What you want is
for all people to be happy, smiling, healthy, cheerful,
greeting one another with real affection, not bogus affection. What you want is for every man to be free, to be
himself, money galore, and salt for horses. But don't try
to do too much for the various domesticated animals, as
they are quite adequately protected by the British. Just
throw in a few kind words now and then for the marsupials, because human beings are killing them off by
trying to make household pets of them. Improve yourself, by all means. Seek out a good Catholic priest and
let him explain to you why your only chance is to go
along with him, but if you can't find a priest, or if he
gives you the brush on his way to a television broadcast,
seek out a good Protestant preacher, a Doctor of Divinity, you might say, and let him smile a benediction upon
your head. But if he tells you you can't lead, tell him he

lies. Some Doctors of Divinity read secular books and you might run into one who happens to have the impertinence to regard your wish to lead with a slightly fishy eye. He may have read somewhere the insulting term *delusion of grandeur* and imagine that it applies to *you*, whereas actually, as any true thinker knows, it only applies to other people. If you find a Doctor of Divinity who isn't with it, strictly from Hicksville, a man who hasn't got it, move along to a Rabbi. Take him into your confidence, but if you want to be really smart, don't take him *entirely* into your confidence, he may not be the sort of trustworthy fellow you think he is. Move out among these professionals, but watch it carefully, always. Keep on your toes, keep moving, in and out, the most devastating tricks are the ones you never suspect are tricks at all, and unless you are careful, instead of proceeding with your leadership you may suddenly find yourself converted to something you don't understand because there is no reasonable way by which it can be understood, and instead of helping humanity you may be only helping yourself, but in such a picayune manner as to be disgusting, by kneeling and praying, for instance: by going out of your way to be humble, a condition you have got to guard against with every ounce of your energy.

Or perhaps, rather than lead, you prefer to follow. I can help you there, too. Stand up, in case you're lying down. Find out where the other followers are. Go on out there and find them and follow—that is *also* for humanity. Cultivate being weak, cultivate knowing who a real follower is, yourself of course, the greatest follower of them all—small, wiry, quick of foot, and almost always never more than the fifth to throw a stone. Be a big follower, a credit to your creed, your color, your na-

tionality, your union, your party, and your God, but
only if your creed is one of the more carefully chosen by
the experts, only if your color is white or off-white, only
if your nationality is big and strong and crooked, only
if your union is run on the superior methods established
by gangsters, only if your party is safe and sound and
with a good long tradition of lying sincerely, and only
if your God is Stanley L. Buster, founder of Cheatism,
Belittlum, Horsery, Antway, Dirtout, and other religious
and philosophical systems. Follow Stan, he's your man.

But perhaps you would rather be neither a leader
nor a follower. You would rather play the violin. Seek
out a nice teacher.

I can, as you see, inspire as effectively as the next
man, if I must. But you may already have been adequately inspired by the experts of America, you may
even have been overinspired.

Have no care, I can also despire you.

Now, of course, I don't need to give you the precise
terms that are employed by the despired upon the in-
spirers, I'm sure you know them, certainly the most
popular and effective of these terms, a matter of two
simple English words, the first a word of four letters and
the second a word of three letters. These two words are
the motto of the despired, and they address them regularly to everybody.

It may very well be that your mother has made you
into a child prodigy. Chess, most likely. The way to become despired at chess is to tip over the board and walk
away. When your mother comes screaming after you,
you reply courteously. (You are never under any cir-
cumstance to speak discourteously to your mother, as
that is not only un-American, it is un-Chinese.)

"Mother," you reply, "*you* play chess, I don't like the

game, it takes too long, and even after I've won, I don't feel any better than I did before I started the game, and what I want to do is feel better, I've got this idea—mad, if you like—that winning a game of chess against a boy from Byelorussia isn't going to help, it isn't going to get it."

If your mother jumps on you, if she mauls you, if she kicks you, knocks you down, well, of course, you understand you can't go out and get yourself another mother, so the sensible thing to do is go home and hit your father. The both of them might as well know you've become despired.

Or if not chess, and if not a child prodigy, perhaps insurance, a year from retirement. Still, it is not too late to become despired, to put aside the arguments of the company and move along to being entirely heedless of the benefits of insurance. It is not too late not to care who is insured and who isn't, or how one poor fool who didn't take out a simple straight policy died a year later and thereby cheated his wife and kids out of an easy ten thousand dollars. It is not too late to cancel your own policy and to be suddenly entirely uninsured, entirely eager not to make a profit from dying and slightly interested in just sitting around and reading the morning paper from cover to cover which you have never before had the time to do. If your wife doesn't like this, kill her. Insure her, kill her, and get her out of the house. Why should she be forever hanging around, lovingly waiting for you to die?

Or if not a child prodigy and chess, or an insurance salesman a year from retirement, perhaps all you are is a bum. Well, there is nothing much I can do for you. You understand being despired as well as I do, perhaps better than I do. Perhaps you're ahead of me. But in

case you're an *inspired* bum because you happened to
read in a thrown-away copy of one of the six inspiring
books that are best sellers every year, in case you want
to improve yourself, button your collar, for instance,
and look for a tie somewhere, and think back to your
early grammar school days when the whole shining
world was yours to take if you had chosen the right road
at the right time, in case the book said you *could* be
more, perhaps *much* more, and you believed the book,
I can help you.

Don't believe the book.

Pass it along to another bum and let *him* believe it.
Pass along the good word, and then sprawl out com-
fortably on the bench in the park. But leap to your feet
if Bernard Baruch comes along. Give him the bench.
He ran up three measly million dollars to thirty
million, over a period of ninety short years, and whenever there was a war he shifted the gears of his hearing
aid from low to high and listened to where the money
was moving, and he got up from the park bench and
went there and a lot of it fell into his hat and he said
to President McKinley, "The only thing we have got to
guard against is the greed of the poor until the economic
cycle has fulfilled itself, a matter of three or four years
at the most, until I have generously added another ten
million to my fortune, always eating sparingly and shift-
ing to low in the presence of crying children who only
believe they are hungry, Mr. President." Always give
that great simple humble humanitarian the bench, he
has been inspired all his life, and he has always been a
leader, not of people but of Presidents, by the nose. He
has always eaten sparingly, and spoken gently to a hundred and seventy million bums who haven't been able
to run a dime up to even *one* million dollars, from sheer

stupidity, overeating, and not having a good hearing aid. Give old Baruch the bench, it's free.

Or if not a child prodigy, or an insurance salesman, or a bum, if something else, if anything else, I can inspire *or* despire, as you prefer. What'll it be? If you haven't got it, I haven't, either, but between us we can get it and then we can quickly give it back, can't we?

Consider yourself inspired, then, or consider yourself despired, and move along. Or consider yourself both inspired and despired, and move along. Huckety buck, the more you put down, the more you pick up. I put down the pieces and now I'm picking them up. My father put down the pieces, too, but he didn't live long enough to pick them up, so I'm picking them up for *him*, too. They're almost harder to pick up than my own, but his father put down his pieces and didn't pick them up, and neither did my father, so you can see there is a lot of picking up that I have got to do if any of us, if any of the Saroyans, no matter what they may be named, are ever going to make sense, and time's running out. We'll probably never make it, but let's be despired about it. Let's *know* we'll never make it, and humanity will just have to get along without ever knowing us or itself whole and true.

8   The Dance

Perhaps you remember the stuff about getting born. It's
all lies. I've written it differently six or seven times. I
write it a little differently every time. How should I
know how it was? If the truth is told, it wasn't me at
all. I wasn't born, I walked in, and there it was, like a
movie. Not the world, that's too big to see with the
naked eye. *Outside* is what it is, and that's where I was,
all dressed of course, and neatly, too. There was outside,
and there I was out with it and in it, not quite three
and not too effective in the matter of knowing and saying my family name.

"Willie," my mother said, but what was the matter
with her voice? And why didn't she say anything more,
as she usually did?

This was a place in Oakland, two hundred miles
north of Fresno, sixty miles north of San Jose where
my father was dead and buried, his poems and notebooks wrapped in the cloth of a flour sack and safely
kept somewhere or other.

I wasn't glad at the time, but after I had done my
time there, after I had done four years there, I was glad
I had been there. It made me know what it is to be
alone, and I decided it had been a good thing that I

had found out almost at the beginning of my life, almost at the beginning of memory, instead of later. The sooner the better in a thing like that. I wept and remembered weeping even as I wept, but I'm glad about that, too.

My mother said, "I must go now and you must not cry. You are a big boy."

Well, of course I was. You don't get any bigger than that at that age. And I was curious about why I was crying. It was rather interesting.

My mother gave me a little toy, and I have written about the toy six or seven times, too. The toy was kept for many years, certainly until I was able to read the name of it: *The Coon Jigger.* It was a wind-up tin man of the kind one sees in a minstrel show, and it jigged on a tin platform. It was really fascinating, but at that time, a time of incredible panic, it seemed spurious, a substitute for something else, a bribe of some kind, and I didn't want it. My mother wound it up and urged me to behold the man jigging, but all I could see was a brightly painted piece of junk that was meant to take the place of something else, something nothing in the world could possibly equal. All the same I watched and listened. I can't say I can still hear the old sound of the tin man dancing, but I can *almost* hear it.

In a play called *The Time of Your Life* I put a young man named Harry the Hoofer. His dancing, his hoofing, his jigging said quite a lot in the play that couldn't be said in any other way. He was the tin dancer of long ago, most likely. I didn't know it when I wrote the play, but it just occurred to me now, twenty-one years later.

And I know a little better now why the dancing of Bojangles made me feel unkillable. He was the jigger liberated from the tin and the machine. And with him I was liberated, too. Bill Robinson, you understand. He

worked on a platform, too, which he reached by strug-
gling with three steps, tap-dancing all the way, a step
forward and then a step back, two forward and two
back, two forward again and one back, but finally he
made it, he arrived, he reached the top of the tin platform of the spurious toy, but Bill Robinson *wasn't* tin,
he was flesh and blood, he was alive. And he could move,
he could dance, he could make his feet do what he
wanted them to do. He could make them speak, he could
make them talk about the human being captured, as I
had once been captured by a small room whose very
smell I felt was deathly, a room with no part of me in it,
in which no part of me could ever be.

And suddenly, after making all manner of sounds
with his voice that weren't quite speech because speech
couldn't say it, he suddenly cried out, "And here I go."
And he went.

And with him I left the deathly room. I left the
orphanage, I went back to Fresno, I went out into the
streets and I fought it out with the wind and the police
and the rain and the fear. Bojangles was in Harry the
Hoofer, and so was the tin toy, and so was Joe Frisco
with his derby, cane, and cigar. And so were all of the
other great dancers I saw in vaudeville.

At a picnic once Lucy Garoghlanian watched the Armenians dancing and then said, "The Saroyans are not
dancers."

The hell you say. They just don't dance with their
feet, that's all, but they love to watch people dance who
can dance that way. Dance? I could barely walk. Joe, in
this same play I'm talking about, said it for me, precisely in those words. This didn't mean something was
the matter with his feet and legs, though. It meant
something else.

Joe Frisco said, "Kid, I can't do it any more."

We were backstage at the Golden Gate in San Francisco. We'd met in a saloon and while he was fetching a cigar I wrote something about his dancing. He read it and said, "You'll get the P-p-p-p-pulitzer prize some day. Come on backstage now, and watch the show."

When we were out on Market Street again he met an old friend and said, "Read this poem the kid wrote about me. I don't know his name, but he's going to win the P-p-p-p-pulitzer prize some day."

"Saroyan," I said.

"Yeah, that's his name. It slipped my mind. He's got me in this poem he wrote."

It wasn't a poem, but that was all right.

I never met Bill Robinson, though. I only saw him offstage two or three times. He was a dancer in the street, too. When he walked it was dancing. I could walk that way, too. It happened when the spirit was sharp. Well, didn't I just say I could barely walk? Of course I did. No contradiction, either. It wasn't often that the spirit was *that* sharp, that's all. I heard him speak in the street, too. He had a voice for talking, and he could laugh, too.

When he died I bought a record of his dancing, of the sounds he always made that were part of his act, the murmurs and chuckles and admonishings, and finally only the speech of dancing, of living.

I listened to the record while I sat and wrote. It helped. A lot of things always helped. Anything that had fear and fight and a need for freedom in it helped. I didn't learn very much about writing from books, certainly not from books that were supposed to tell somebody how to write, I learned a little from what other writers had written, but mainly I learned from other things, from things I saw and heard in the streets, and in the theatres.

She went off, taking with her the smell of mother, and to a man not yet three that's quite a smell. It's made of skin and soap and a little perspiration and a little powder from Woolworth's, but mainly of her, unaccountable, of the pieces broken and not picked up. She knew I wouldn't make a scene. I saw her go, and I saw the door close behind her, and then I saw the tin dancer dancing on the tin platform.

Lies? All lies? Well, I was there, and I was behaving, not for the place, not for the law and order of the place, but for myself, because before the tin dancer had run down I had decided there was nothing to be had from crying, I had stopped crying, and I had decided to wait and see and make do. I decided to figure it out, not for my mother, not for my family, not for my name, but for myself.

The Superintendent came into the room, and I was ready for him. He told me I would go with him to the dormitory for small boys. I went. He was O.K. Later, I gathered he believed I was O.K., too. But I warned you to watch it. I'll go along easily, and all of a sudden I'll make out as if it were something. I was a small boy alone who couldn't say his family name. The size of my eyes increased quite a bit that day.

It wasn't home. It was nothing and nowhere. But it was a little less nothing and nowhere when my brother showed up and we stood and talked, and it was still less nothing when I learned that both of my sisters were in the girls' dormitory and we'd be seeing them from time to time. What a thing it is for a small boy to have an older brother. What a thing it is to have two older sisters.

What a thing it is to be visited for an hour on a Sunday afternoon by a mother, to sit on the grass of the hillside overlooking San Francisco Bay and eat the picnic she has brought from San Francisco, where she has taken a job as a housekeeper and cook for a nice family. What an unbelievable thing it is to be all together for a moment, seeing each other, hearing talk about so many things. When my oldest sister spoke in Armenian to my mother, speaking especially softly, I believed it must be something secret, about us. My mother listened carefully and then replied softly in Armenian.

And then in English she said, "Willie, you want mustard on this ham sandwich?"

I watched her spread the mustard and shut the bun and hand it to me, and then I just ate it, that's all.

Well, if a lot was lost, or at any rate misplaced, *all* wasn't. Still, nothing seemed especially definite, and I asked my brother why she didn't come *every* afternoon. He explained why and although I didn't understand, I *did* understand that there *was* a reason. I sometimes believed we would never see her again and I said so, but my brother said we would, probably. Then, why didn't we see my father again? He said that that was different, he was dead. Even so, why didn't we see him again? He explained why. He did the best a six-year-old could do speaking to a three-year-old. He said we could never expect to see my father again, but I didn't believe that. Hadn't we just seen my mother again, after she had gone away that way? Why shouldn't we see my father again? Dead, my brother said. Didn't mean a thing. Wasn't my mother dead, too? Then, how did we just see her again?

"Sticks and stones can break my bones but names can never hurt me." The older boys, quarreling, had shouted the remark at one another. What sticks? What stones? What bones? What names? Nobody used a stick and nobody used a stone. No bones were broken, but *something* hurt. And it *wasn't* me. It was something else. Perhaps everything else. There was a hurt in everything. And it was always looking to be healed, but from the faces of everybody I ever saw it *wasn't* being healed.

Two of the boys of the seven who slept in the room where I slept cried in the dark every night. I listened to them, and wished them healing. I knew it was worse for them. It *had* to be. In the daylight they tried to pretend they hadn't cried. Of the five who never cried a few teased them, but not me, I fought the ones who teased them. The two who cried had nobody. That's the way I figured it. They might actually have had a mother somewhere or a father or a brother or a sister, but I figured they had nobody. They were entirely alone. They were so alone they couldn't wait for lights out to let themselves go. It happens to kids in big families, even. Surrounded by love even, some kids are entirely alone, and it hurts, it makes them cry in the dark, God love and protect them.

9 The Reader

Love of paper is the important thing, after love of honor, most likely. Honor is impossible not to love but inevitable to betray. It is when the betrayal of honor does not mortify a man that he may be said to be adult. A truly honorable man has got to sit, as Joe sat in *The Time of Your Life,* or, as it was known to me when I was writing it, *The Light Fantastic.*

George Jean Nathan's name for it was *The Sunset Sonata,* but that sounded too much like Strindberg for me.

I saw a statue of him in Stockholm one day, and one day I read an excerpt somewhat about him from an auto-biography by Osbert Sitwell that had been given the name of *The Man Who Drove Strindberg Mad.*

This was a small boy who rang the doorbell of Strind-berg's house and then ran off to hide and watch Strind-berg stand in the doorway, puzzled. Later the boy be-came a bore to whom things were kind, as they are not kind to the rest of us. Bells can be very unkind. Strind-berg's doorbell was very unkind to him, but of course it was this boy.

The reason an honorable man must sit is that if he gets up and walks he may hurt somebody, but that's put-ting it poorly. Joe is thirty-one in the play, although he has always been played by somebody who has been over

fifty, but that's all right. Joe is thirty-one because I was
thirty-one when I wrote the play, it's as simple as that.
At thirty-one if you don't know what hurts people you're
not very likely to know at thirty-two.

People hurt people, although things frequently seem
to hurt them too, but after you investigate a little you
discover that it was the action of people upon the things
that actually did the hurting: the boy who rang Strind-
berg's doorbell, not the bell itself, for instance.

Joe didn't want to hurt people. He was so determined
not to, he sat all the time. But even then, he discovered
that he hurt them. Even when he tried to help them he
discovered that he hurt them. To sit wasn't it, either,
so he got up and left the saloon and the curtain came
down and the play ended. It was written on paper,
which I have always loved, and I have no trouble knowing why, either.

My mother brought out the bundle of my father's
writings when I asked if I might look at them. I was
nine or ten and we were back in Fresno, in our own
rented house on San Benito Avenue. This was an important event in my life, I may say. First, I was a little
surprised that my mother had carefully kept something
of my father's, for it had seemed a long time since he
had come and gone, and what was the good of keeping
worthless stuff like an unknown writer's writings, the
writer himself long absent from a world that had moved
along swiftly? Second, I was pleased that she believed I
deserved to have a look at the stuff.

"There was more," she said. "He lost some, we lost
some, this is all that remains." In Armenian, you understand: English was spoken only in the presence of those
who were unable to speak Armenian.

She untied the knots in the cloth and spread out the

ends so that all that was there might be seen as a whole: a stack of home-made notebooks and manuscripts.

"You will notice that he made notebooks out of wrapping paper." She went back to her work in the kitchen.

I was an hour trying to understand the stuff. It was an hour like forever, if that means anything. This was not like the books in his small library, this was himself. Living, he had made these notebooks and manuscripts out of butcher paper, store paper, any kind of paper that had happened to come his way, and then he himself had written upon the paper. The stuff was dated, and most of it was written before I was born. His library was made up of books he had bought in connection with being a preacher. His name was written in each book, where he was, and what year it was. He left no book related to his being a writer of poetry. That was his own, something he may even have felt a little guilty about, as if the writing of a poem might be said to be frivolous.

In 1919 when I was ten going on eleven I believed the world couldn't fool me. I had found out about it moving through the streets with papers to sell, sitting in the movie and vaudeville theatres, sometimes to see a whole show, sometimes to see half, but now and then to catch only a favorite act of vaudeville, or a part in a movie that made me feel good. I had ways of getting into the theatres without paying: if I didn't know the ticket-taker, I knew how to sneak it.

The time between the tin dancer at the orphanage and the end of the war on November 11, 1918, was the fullest time in my life. The few early dead in my family had been followed by an assortment of more recent dead. My father was only the first in a short line of family dead and a long line of others dead. He was not alone

on that side of the picture. By 1919 I had come to feel
old and wise, as perhaps I had a right to feel, as perhaps
I was, in fact. I felt older than my father had *ever* been,
as a matter of fact. The world had bullied him, I felt,
and it hadn't bullied me, and never would.

I was a runner and he had been above running. I ran
to everything, especially to the extra editions of *The
Evening Herald* which near the end of the war came out
during the school lunch hour, so that a swift runner
could get his papers, sell them, earn a dollar and be back
before the school bell rang for the start of the afternoon
classes. Eating was a matter of no importance at a time
like that. I had made a good name as a hustler, I had
one of the best corners in town, I had always been able
to sell more papers than the other newsboys, excepting
three or four. Mr. York, the street sales manager, liked
me and I liked him, most of all for letting me start selling papers in the first place when he knew I was probably not even eight, let alone ten, which was supposed
to be the minimum age permissible.

He once spoke to me as if I were his own age, with
his own understanding. He had come to my corner to
see if I needed any more papers when two half-drunk
Indians began to see about killing one another and were
stopped by two cops and taken away in a patrol wagon.

"Who knows why brothers fight, Willie? You and
Henry fight, don't you? I always fought *my* brothers."

At first I hadn't believed they *were* brothers. They
hadn't looked enough alike to be brothers, and then
suddenly, just before I was about to say so, I understood
what he meant. Of course they weren't brothers, but
they might as well have been for the bitterness of their
fighting, two bewildered, confused, stunned, lost men of

another time and place wandering around in a city full of strangers. They couldn't fight the people in the town, so they fought one another. The fight was a protest against the new people, who had no connection with the Indians. The stores were full of stuff they could never use, that had nothing to do with the way they had always lived. They had had a bottle of whisky and they had drunk from it by turns, openly, in full sight of the people and the police, but they had been left to themselves, and so they had finally fallen upon one another on my corner, the almost-empty bottle on the curb near Huff's Popcorn Wagon, carefully set there by the last drinker just before the start of the fight. Huff picked up the bottle during the fight and put it back after the fight. It stayed there as if it were to remain the property of the Indians forever, but just before closing for the night old man Huff picked it up, and drank it empty, and then put the bottle away in the wagon, and went off.

I knew the world, and it stank, and I loved it. I ran to it every day, and to the people in it, who also stank. I believed my father hadn't known the world, he had known something else.

I picked up the first notebook and just held it a moment. And then I read the stuff my father had written on the cover. It doesn't matter what the stuff actually was, I can't be sure of it, but I can be sure that after the name of it came his name, very clearly, in English, with that touch of foreignness which is in the handwriting of all men who are not English or American by birth.

The Word, we'll say. *A Poem, by Armenak Saroyan. The Bowery, New York, June, 1905,* we'll say.

I know he lived in the Bowery for some time. I know
he reached New York in 1905, alone.

I read the poem, or at any rate as much of it as I
could take at that age, and then I put the thing aside
and had a look at the next notebook. I sat and studied
the stuff an hour that seemed years, certainly all of the
years from 1908 to 1919, all of the years of my life, and
the last six of his. This this this is what's left: failure,
loss, finality. On wrapping paper or butcher's paper or
any old kind of paper a man might write upon which
did not need to be paid for.

He hadn't made it. But as if as a special favor to me
he had kept a record of it, of the failure, the loss, and
the finality, and there I was at the round table in the
dining room, his only reader.

The stuff in Armenian I couldn't read, so I looked at
it and tried to believe it was his best stuff, much better
than the stuff in English, which was probably not quite
as useless as I believed it was at the time, not quite as
foolish, not quite as unnecessary.

In a sense the writing was my own, and I didn't like
it. It just wasn't tough enough for the truth of us, of
this world, and I wished it had been. There wasn't
enough of it, either, and everything stopped before it
was finished. Nothing was finished, not even a short
poem. He'd needed time, and a place, and he'd had
neither. But instead of being mad at others, or at the
world, the stuff made me mad at him. "You should have
been able to do better than that," but I didn't mean the
writing alone, I meant the living, and the early disappearance. I certainly didn't mean the notebooks he'd
made. I admired them. I loved the plain paper which
had held up so well, which had never been meant to be

written upon, and I loved the ink with which he had made his words, and the words themselves, the calligraphy, the sensible spacing, the clarity, everything except the meaning of the words: failure, loss, and finality.

"*He* didn't make it, *I'll* make it. When he and I wrote that time we didn't make it because he was alone, but now he's not and we'll make it. I'll *buy* my paper, I won't fold a big piece of butcher's paper into a notebook, I'll pay a dime for a ready-made one, and I'll write in it."

I became bored with the debris, and went to the kitchen for a long drink from the faucet.

"Well?" my mother said as if she might have been waiting for years to hear a verdict.

"It's amazing," I said. *Zarmanali* is the Armenian word. I didn't want to go any further. I didn't want to explain *how* it was amazing.

"He didn't have time enough," she said.

She tied up the bundle again and put it back with the other stuff she kept of that kind.

I walked to town, to the Public Library on a Sunday afternoon in the winter, and wandered around in there thinking about all of the books of all of the others who had written stuff. Was their stuff any better than his stuff, actually? Well, of course some of it was, but most of it wasn't, most of it was simply finished, each writer had had time enough and he had seen the thing through, as useless as that was, and although the stuff was in books and on the shelves of the Public Library, nobody was reading it.

Well, somebody was reading my father's stuff. I was.

I mentioned the stuff to my brother, but he wasn't interested. We may not have had a fight about it, but

we had a fight about something, and as always my
mother came to the back door and said very clearly,
"Have you gone savage again?" Whereupon we stopped,
as we always did. In Armenian it's a matter of only two
words, and the two words say it better than the five of
English by which I have tried to translate them. *Got-
khak noren?* And as always we didn't speak to one another for a little while, both of us ashamed, each of us
angry at himself. But soon we spoke again, as if we
hadn't had another stupid fight.

"What else did he leave?" I asked my mother. She
said he had bought the six cane chairs with the rattan
seats the year before his death, and there they were in
the house as good as ever, or almost as good. A man from
Chinatown had put in new rattan seats twice, but when
he failed to show up again we bought cardboard seats
from Woolworth's and tacked them over the broken
rattan. Somewhere along the line somebody painted
them, and then in 1939, after the opening of *The Time
of Your Life* in New York, I began to scrape off the
paint, to get them back the way they had been when
he had bought them, but I never finished the job. You
never do. No matter what the job is, something comes
along and stops you.

Whenever nobody was standing at the door, after the
bell had rung and Strindberg had opened the door,
Strindberg had imagined no bell had actually rung and
believed he was going mad. Well, it isn't that he was
mistaken about going mad, it's just that there was a perfectly sensible explanation for the ringing of the bell
but nobody at the door. The boy was ringing the bell
and hiding, that's all. He was having fun driving Strind-
berg mad, but Strindberg was ahead of him, he was there
already, and all he needed was the accident of this boy

being in his neighborhood instead of in the neighborhood of a man like the man the boy grew up to be, a man who would have been so sure of himself as to know somebody was being a cut-up, lay for him, catch him, and change his character slightly with two quick clobbers on the head.

You betray honor, you betray yourself, you betray the human race when you believe the way to truth is the way taken by the mob, when you agree because it's convenient, when you accept, when you conform, when you don't go after truth as if it had never before been seized. And by the mob I mean you and your brother not fighting each other any more in protest to the arrival of the grand lie, because now you are grown-up and know better, know it's useless, who needs to love anything that much any more? Who needs to love paper, language, honor, or the hope of love any more?

His voice quavering as it did when he was speaking on purpose, George Jean Nathan said on the radio, "In one short year of the American theatre his name has been made and his pockets lined with gold." I was driving home to San Francisco from New York when I heard him. I liked the *lined with gold* part best because it was so old-fashioned and unexpected. I hadn't heard any other living man use the expression.

Back in New York, at a corner table at 21, he said, "I like your new play, *Love's Old Sweet Song,* and I know just the man for the Greek wrestler. Herbert Hoover." He was always drawing up special casts for my plays and once urged me to wire Stalin to play the part of the grandmother in a revival of *My Heart's in the Highlands,* because I had mentioned that my grandmother Lucy resembled Stalin.

When I visited H. L. Mencken at his home in Balti-

more and invited him to come and see a performance of
Love's Old Sweet Song, Mencken puffed at his cigar and
said, "I never go to the theatre. I can't stand the boobs."

"The audience?"

"Oh, no," Mencken said, *they're* charming. I mean
on the stage."

10   The Clown

If you want somebody you know and love to become a very nice guy, a very attractive nonentity, a courteous young man at all times, or a car thief, a junky, a maniac on a motorcycle, give him letters of introduction to all of the people he thinks he wants to meet in connection with the work he thinks he wants to do. He will make out just fine. Let a boy have the good strong love and regard of a father, or a friend of a father or a friend of a mother, and let him carry letters of introduction to important people wherever he goes, and that boy will make out just fine, if he was going to in any case, and maybe even if he wasn't going to in any case.

My mother's kid brother Aram, the success, or Aram the Successful, the Criminal Lawyer, the Grape Shipper, the Vineyardist, the Orator, the National Patriot, was quite simply on the one hand the greatest man in my family insofar as making out in the world was concerned, and on the other the most arrogant, impatient, irritable, unreasonable, unpredictable, and generally preposterous man I had ever met. All the same I liked him, and died laughing (as we used to say) at the stories he told, which were and probably always will be the funniest I have ever heard, told with the greatest possible style, control, and timing. I in turn enjoyed killing him with my imitations of all kinds of pomposity, including his own, especially in oratory. He was swift, hearty, excited, and always busy. He was wise in the ways of the world, he had an instinct about business, from poverty he had moved to wealth in a matter of less than ten years in the new world. He spoke English with an accent and liked to throw around such legal terms as *every way, shape, manner, and form; irrelevant, immaterial, and out of order;* and so on. Now and then he even threw out a *prima facie* and a *non compis mentis.*

I met him pretty much for the first time when I left the orphanage, and my mother and her four kids were together in our own home, which he visited early one evening. He began killing everybody, talking swiftly, laughing, and scarcely noticing anybody but always aware of their astonished noticing of him.

We were in a bare little kitchen for the warmth from the stove, and I was seated on an apple box, fascinated but also a little confused. He was Uncle Aram, I knew *that,* and he was in the family, but I didn't know he was my mother's kid brother.

All of a sudden, speaking swift Armenian which I hadn't quite picked up in the three or four days I had been home, he said, "Willie, shut the door."

Now, I had been brought up in the orphanage according to rules that hadn't yet been displaced. At the orphanage an order of that kind would be given only to the person who had been responsible for the condition to be corrected, the person who, in this case, had *opened* the door, and I certainly hadn't. I don't know who had come in last. It was probably Aram himself.

In the meager Armenian that I could manage by which to make the reply that was required I said the equivalent of, "Me wasn't opener."

I meant the reply righteously, without any kind of comic implication, but the effect of it on him was hilarious and entirely unexpected.

First, he said very quickly and softly, "Very well, you weren't the opener—be the shutter."

And then he roared with the loudest laughter I had ever heard, both at my garbled remark and his brilliant reply.

There was nothing for it, as the English say. I shut the door, hearing the laughter of everybody in the kitchen: my mother, my sisters, my brother, and this strange man, then probably no more than twenty-three, but to me a very old man.

The laughter was contagious. It was necessary for me to react to it by being glad about whatever the joke was, but at the same time the laughter had the effect of making me walk as if I really didn't know how—a walk of confusion, embarrassment, foolishness, of having been unwittingly captured without having known it was possible under the circumstances, but at the same time a walk out of a feeling of having been amusing, of having caused laughter. And so while I had no real control over the way I was moving I felt glad that it was the way it was, I felt pleased to have been taken for a comic, which I was not. This wasn't exactly a new experience, it had happened before, at the orphanage and at school.

A serious man can frequently find himself seeming to be awfully funny to others who aren't serious, who aren't occupying the same dimension of the human experience that he is occupying, not by choice but inevitably. At the orphanage most of the adults tried not to call on me to answer a moral question in company, to illustrate a point of some kind, because invariably I didn't help them very much, not because I didn't want to, or disliked the point they meant to make, but because it never seemed to turn out that way. No matter what I replied, everybody burst into laughter, and my posture and walk were affected in the manner I have just described. Why? My voice wasn't anything at all like a funny voice, high-pitched, for instance. I didn't stammer, I didn't start a sentence and abandon it and start again, or repeat the same thing over. I simply said what I had to say, which always seemed to me the only thing that could possibly be said, and yet every time I did so there was laughter and sometimes pandemonium, with the adults deliberately choosing not to stop it for a moment or two, taking part in it, in fact.

As for myself, I was both surprised and pleased, because it is good to hear laughter, but as far as I was able to understand anything there was nothing funny in what I had said. In time, though, as we would have to expect, most likely, I made the most of the situation and took to being amusing on purpose.

But the earnestness that was with me, that was forever at work within me, did not diminish on that account. If anything it was increased, and so when I heard that clowns were all deeply serious men, I had already suspected as much.

I liked Shaw especially for his clowning, because I knew something else was going on at the same time, and I believed it was something of importance to everybody who had found out a little about him because of his clowning, and to everybody else, too.

When we met our talk came around at length to the pose, any man's pose, every man's, and in this connection I remarked that from the time a week ago that I had accepted his kind invitation to visit him I had been reading around in Hesketh Pearson's biography, which, as he knew, had as much in it written by Shaw himself about himself, or the pose of himself, as by Pearson.

I said, "He did what he could under the circumstances, I suppose, and it's a pleasant book, a pleasant life, but I don't get the feeling that it's about you. If you don't mind, Pearson's Shaw isn't half the man you are. He missed the boat, and you helped him."

Shaw didn't laugh at this, and after a moment he said quite earnestly something I at first believed was more of his famous wit, but it was no such thing, he was thinking in another dimension.

"I helped him all I *could*," he said, and it was all I could do not to break into laughter.

"You helped your biographer to make you seem less than you are?" I thought. But that wasn't what Shaw meant at all. He meant that he literally did all that he could that he believed would be helpful to his biographer, and either Pearson was the wrong man for the job (which I knew Shaw had insisted on), or Shaw himself, for all his intelligence, or affectation of it, didn't really know who he was.

In any case, with that beginning with Aram, the business of the open door, and who was eligible or obliged to shut it, it was probably inevitable that Aram and I would have a lot of laughs together, and so of course it came to pass, although as I grew older and saw into more things more accurately we had fallings out, and sometimes they were loud and unintentially funny.

11   The Fire

When I was seventeen, for instance, I wanted to get out of town because I seemed to be fighting everybody. I had been kicked out of school so many times that I finally left for good when I was fifteen and went to work with Mexicans and Japanese on one of Aram's vineyards, which he owned jointly with his brother-in-law, Dikran Bagdasarian, who had married Aram's sister Verkine.

At every school I had ever gone to I had fought everybody: the teachers, the principals, and the classmates who were bullies, snobs, or crooks: Emerson, Longfellow, Tech High (where I had learned typing and shorthand, but never used the shorthand, not even as a writer, as I had read that Dickens had), and finally Fresno High.

I had fought my mother after the age of eleven about Sunday School, cutting the lawn, helping with the dishes, behavior in general, and by reading every minute that I was free to read, after work when there were no games going on in the neighborhood.

Once or twice I believe she said it was harmful to the mind to read so much, especially such big and surely serious books, probably full of all manner of evil. Certainly others in the family had told me the same thing many times. Now, it isn't to be presumed that reading cannot possibly be harmful, for of course it can be, anything can be, so that what they were really saying was either, "Wait a while, you're too young for every book in the Public Library," or "Don't go out there, it's deep, it's dangerous, you could drown."

Some of the stuff did in fact trouble me. I remember, for instance, a book called *Criminality in Children,* which astonished me, for I could not believe any child could possibly be criminal, and yet the book was full of case histories.

I knew kids, I had known a lot of them at their most vulnerable, at the orphanage, and there wasn't a criminal in the lot, or anyone even remotely resembling a criminal.

There were runaways, but why wouldn't there be? The place wasn't home. I ran away myself, twice with two other boys my age, and once alone, but we always became hungry and afraid of either greater homelessness than the homelessness at the orphanage, or of being stopped by some busybody and turned over to the police, in which event we would get it, as the saying was.

There were fights, too, but again why wouldn't there be? I was provoked into a fight with Sammy Isaacs, for instance, who in turn was also provoked—a little amusement for boys of nine or ten, but not criminality. The older boys actually convinced us we *had* to fight because of invented insults passed by each of us when the back of the other had been turned, and so at the age of five or six, I kept waiting for my best friend to strike the first blow and he kept waiting for me to do so, and finally it happened, although I don't remember who struck the first blow, perhaps we were pushed together, and we began to strike and at the same time to cry, while the older boys laughed and called out to us by name, telling us what to do next.

"In the nose, Willie, in the nose."

"In the eye, Sammy, in the eye."

And so on. Ten minutes later, far from the older boys, we stood together and talked soberly about something else entirely, the fight an unaccountable fantasy of some kind.

And once, two or three boys of twelve or thirteen deliberately set fire to the steps of the Administration Building, at night. This was a prank, pure and simple, a protest against the parade of pomposities up and down the steps: the members of the Board of Directors, the various preachers and their wives, and other adults who belonged. It wasn't arson.

In any case, the fire was unsuccessful: they had put a lighted match to a copy of the *Oakland Tribune,* but the paper had burned itself out before the fire had moved up into the wood of the steps. There was a lot of smoke, though, and upon the discovery of the embers of the newspaper, and the arsonist plot, so to put it, there was a lot of official hysteria.

The whole place was instantly transformed into a penitentiary. All privileges suspended. Everybody confined to his dormitory. No talking, while the investigation was made. Only reading or school work. The investigation went on and on, past the time for supper, driving the Irish cook a little berserk. And yet the culprits remained unknown.

At last, an hour and a half past suppertime, when even the smallest boy knew who the three boys were but wouldn't squeal if it cost him his life, or so each of us *thought,* at any rate: at last the announcement went through the whole orphanage: There will be no supper until the guilty persons, boys or girls, present themselves to the Superintendent.

Slowly, another half hour went by. Every now and then the three boys glanced at one another, hoping not to be observed by the matrons and the Superintendent, who were moving around, watching everybody.

What were the three boys going to do? If they held out, I thought, we might all be forced to make a break for freedom, and perhaps even if we got caught, the police would take our side, since we had not been given supper. It would be a good thing if the boys didn't confess, and the management of the orphanage tried to get us to bed without supper, because most likely they would fail. There would be a break. I was all for it, but at the same time I was also all for the meat pie which we knew was for supper, a favorite with everybody, and the pride of the Irish cook who by now was sneaking drinks and speaking under her breath about the evil souls who were tormenting the dear children.

Two or three times I noticed the three boys exchanging glances, and for that matter exchanging silent messages, too. Why should the *three* of them confess and get a beating? Wouldn't it be wiser if the oldest of them protected the other two? Or wouldn't it be more equitable if the one who had come up with the idea stepped forward and said he alone had done it? At an orphanage this kind of silent talking goes on all the time, as in fact it does among any group that is held in bondage.

At last it was agreed among them, because the silent message was out to everybody, and suddenly Melvin Athey, fourteen, and the oldest of the boys, got to his feet, stepped up to Mr. Hagen, the Superintendent, and said, "Sir, I did it."

A cheer went up immediately, both in the Boys' Dormitory, and in the Girls'. The Superintendent went off with Melvin, and after a minute or two the announcement was made that supper would be in five minutes, everybody wash, and fall in line for the entrance into the dining room.

But there was no *criminality* in anybody at the orphanage.

Consequently, I didn't know what to make of the case histories in the book. I tended to believe whatever happened to be in print, in a book, because I felt it had been permitted to appear in print, in a book, because it was true. Well, some of the kids in the book *were* criminals. Now, how could that be? It made a problem for me, for my thinking, for what I believed about kids: namely, that they were directed or pushed into their earliest behavior by conditions, which of course *they* hadn't made.

12   The Poem

I had fought everybody for so long at school, at home,
and everywhere else that I was sick of it, and sick of myself. I believed the way to become healed was to get out
of town.

It was July, 1926.

Soon I'd be eighteen years old, but still I was in
Fresno, which I now hated.

I went up to Aram's office to see about getting paid
for the occasional office work I had done for a year or
more, which I can't pretend I had especially *minded*
doing, which in fact I had enjoyed doing. It had been
better than nothing, so to say, but at the same time I
had actually written a great many letters for him on the
typewriter, I had run errands for him, I had announced
his clients, I had asked them to wait when he was busy,
and in general I had made myself useful.

Still, he hadn't ever handed me any money, except
when he had sent me out for a cold watermelon from
Long John, or a pound of pistachio nuts, or a leg of
lamb for him to take home. Even when I had handed
him the change he had invariably accepted all of it.

He was alone in his office when he looked up and
saw me. I couldn't help noticing that he knew my visit
was not a routine one. And I knew he was ready for me.

"Sit down," he said. "What's on your mind?"

"I want to get out of town."

"I think that's a good idea. You've been giving my sister a bad time long enough. Get out and stay out. When are you leaving?"

"Right away, but I haven't got any money."

"You don't need any money. Bums don't need any money. Go out to the S.P. and grab a freight, the way all the bums do."

"I thought you might pay me."

"For what?"

"For the work I did for you."

"Work *you* did for *me?* This place has been a college for you. You should pay me."

"Well, maybe, then, you'd *lend* me five dollars."

Well, here, for some reason, he went a little berserk, shouting first in English, then in Armenian, and finally in Turkish and Kurdish.

His voice was being heard all over the Rowell Building. The dentist next door stuck his head into the office expecting to say he had a very delicate piece of work to do and Aram was disturbing his patient, but Aram shouted at him before he could open his mouth, which soon enough fell open with astonishment.

"Get out, you dentist. Don't come into this office. This is a place of business. Get back where you belong, and drill your rotten teeth."

And now he felt required to imitate the sound of the drill, saying, "Bzzzz, bzzzz, bzzzz, all day long. Open wider, please. Wider, please. Bzzzz, bzzzz, bzzzz. Get out of here with your dainty little washed hands."

The instant the dentist's face disappeared, before the door was even fully shut, he came right back at me.

Inside, in spite of the anger I felt, I was laughing, because the man was crazy, but very funny.

Now, though, when he renewed the attack, I couldn't take it in silence any more, and I began to shout back at him, only louder than he was shouting.

"For God's sake, what kind of a man are you, anyway? You made a fortune last year and you're going to make a bigger fortune this year. I worked for you. Every penny I've ever earned I gave to my mother. I can't go to her and ask her for money. What are you shouting at me for?"

Now, after I said each of these things, he shouted a nullifying reply, making a kind of ridiculous duet.

All of the windows on the court of the Rowell Building were being lifted by typists, bookkeepers, dentists, lawyers, fruit shippers, and others, and everybody knew who was shouting: the Armenians, the Saroyans, Aram and his nephew Willie.

When I said, "For God's sake, what kind of a man are you?", Aram said, "A great man, you jackass, not a jackass like you."

"You made a fortune last year."

"Bet your life I did, more than you or anybody else will ever know."

"And you're going to make a bigger fortune this year."

"The biggest yet in every way, shape, manner and form."

"I worked for you."

"You *shit—that's* what you did."

"Every penny I've ever earned I gave to my mother."

"That poor girl has been driven mad by your foolishness. You want to be a writer. Get money in a bank and

write *checks,* that's the way to be a writer. That's the
kind of writer *I* am, not a stupid poem writer. *The
moon is sinking in the sea.* The moon is sinking in your
empty head, that's where the moon is sinking. (This of
course was his swiftest idea of poetry, and of course
there's no telling where he had gotten it from.) You
gave her a few pennies, so you could eat six or seven
times a day, and sleep in a warm bed in your own room,
and get free hotel service. Don't talk to me about giving
my sister money. Your *pennies?"*

"I can't go to her and ask her for money."

"Bet your life you can't. You've got to go to the bank
for money, the way I do. Tell them what you want it
for—to be a bum—and they'll give it to you. But if they
don't, they'll give you a blotter. You can always use a
blotter, can't you?"

"What are you shouting at me for?"

"Because you're a disgrace to my family. To my sister.
To the Saroyan family. Now, get out of here."

For some reason all of a sudden I thought of my father. Surely nobody had ever spoken to him that way, if
in fact anybody had ever shouted at him, but I got the
feeling that they had actually. Who wanted *The moon is
sinking in the sea?* Who wanted any part of such nonsense? This was America. This was California. This was
Fresno. This was the real world, not the world of the
moon and the sea.

I knew I wasn't going to get any money, so there was
no point in shouting any more. I just didn't know how
to get money, even money I had earned, or at any rate
believed I had earned, but perhaps I was mistaken, perhaps he was right, perhaps I owed him money for having
gone to college in his office, and so the first thing I must
do is earn some money and pay him. It didn't help at

all that he was famous all over town as the most open-handed man of wealth among the Armenians. He donated, officially, to everything that came along, and he made generous hand-outs to all kinds of needy Armenians because they knew how to get money from him. They knew how to get him to write a check, and they always cried out with feigned astonishment, "A hundred dollars, Aram? Really, I had hoped for no more than ten."

Hushed, earnest, a little astonished, but still respectful, I left his office and sneaked out of the building, taking the stairs so I wouldn't have to face the elevator operator or anybody who might be in the elevator.

13   The Ride

I went to the garage of the Californian Hotel and asked
the man there if he knew of anybody driving out of
town. He said somebody at the hotel had asked to have
his car ready at nine, but it wasn't six yet.

I said I'd wait, and I did, which is never much fun
and at that time was none at all. At last a bellboy
brought the man's bags across the street from the hotel
to the garage, and there was the man himself. He was
just fine, but all of a sudden I didn't think I ought to
speak to him, even. If I didn't, though, what then? I
couldn't go home again. But if I asked for a ride, he
might turn me down, and I'd been turned down enough
for one day.

He was a well-dressed, successful-looking man of forty
or so who was smoking a nickel cigar, a salesman of some
kind, and he was all right, but I just didn't want to risk
another humiliation.

In any case, he'd *seen* me, and he knew perfectly well
I wanted a ride out of town, wherever hc was going, so
why didn't he say something?

I was hungry, I felt desperate and cut off from everything I had ever been related to, but I wanted to be
snappy and smart like so many guys in the movies I had

seen, a maker of laughter, somebody anybody would be glad to have along for a ten-hour drive somewhere. I *wanted* to, but I couldn't. This just wasn't a movie, it was me.

At last I decided I'd have to risk it, that's all. By three or four or five in the morning I'd be out of town at last, and on my own.

I went around to where I'd be able to see the man, and he'd be able to see me, and with the driest mouth I have ever had I said, "I'm looking for a ride. Anywhere."

But before I had finished speaking I knew it had happened again. I'd been turned down. The man didn't even answer me. I wanted to walk away quickly, but that would have been too humiliating. It would be better to just hang around, not facing him any more, until he drove off.

I'd have to try the S.P., after all. I turned away and pretended to be interested in the hood of the parked car directly in front of me. I heard the motor start and felt deeply relieved. The motor was raced a couple of times, and then I heard the man call out, "O.K., kid. Hop in. It's a long way to San Francisco."

I was about to run, but suddenly I had to check it.

"I'm going to Los Angeles," I said.

The man puffed at his cigar. "You said anywhere."

"Anywhere *south.*"

He puffed again, and drove off.

I was about to start walking to the S.P. when the same bellboy came along with some more bags, and with him this time was a little old man who came straight up to me and said, "You want a ride, I'm going to Los Angeles."

He stopped in Bakersfield and asked me to have a sandwich and a cup of coffee with him.

"I haven't got any money."

"I know that. You'll have a dollar in your pocket when we get to Los Angeles, too, and forget it."

We reached Los Angeles a little before daybreak. I got out of the car in the heart of town and said, "I'll never forget this."

"Forget it, I said." And he was gone.

And there all around me was this strange silent city that I hadn't had in mind at all. I had had San Francisco in mind. I was awfully tired, but keyed up, too. I walked around and saw some coffee shops that were open, but I didn't go in because I didn't want to break the silver dollar until I had to. I found a water fountain and had a long drink, and a half hour later went back and had another one. I felt beat and mean, but at the same time exhilarated and glad. At least I'd *started*, thanks to the good luck of running into the little old man.

He's been dead for years, most likely, but even if he weren't, he wouldn't know what he did for me, although we talked all the way from Fresno to Los Angeles. I must have told him quite a lot about myself, from which, I mean, he *might* have gathered that he had done me a great, an unexpected, an incredible kindness.

14 The Job

When the stores opened I went to a big department store called Bullock's and asked for a job. I got one in the shipping department, or perhaps the proper term for it would be the delivery department. It was about a mile from the store, and on my way there I stopped for a cup of coffee and a doughnut. When I got there I went straight to work, standing at a moving belt down which packages came addressed to different parts of town. My job was to lift them and put them in various marked bins. It was stupid work, but it was work.

But this isn't about that job, that visit to Los Angeles, this is about having it easy, having members of your family send you along wherever you want to go with letters of introduction to people who might be pleased to have you go to work for them.

I worked three days but I didn't feel strong on the third day, and on the fourth I couldn't work any more. I didn't *say* so, the foreman noticed it. He said I'd better go home, better take my pay, though, so he could have back the two dollars he had loaned me, but I could have the job back as soon as I was O.K. again.

I took the money and went to my room in a kind of rooming house just back of the big new Public Library, and I went to bed. I didn't know sickness at all, believed

it was a flaw of character, saw no excuse for it, didn't
realize I had a high fever, just ached and went down the
hall and drank flat tasteless water and went back to bed
and went through hell, the hell of my stupid life, and
waited, and went down the hall again and ran a bath
and got in and went back to bed and sweated and fell
into fighting sleep and woke up drenched and put on
my clothes and went out and bought a dime's worth of
grapes and ate them and could barely stand and went
back and believed the room was a coffin and got back in
bed and waited.

After three days the worst was over, the landlady
wanted her money, I paid her, and she said I wouldn't
have to leave the room until six that night. Now, all I
had was thirty or forty cents, so I walked around town
and tried to think. I found a recruiting tent for the National Guard in a little park in the heart of town and
asked the man in uniform what it was all about.

You had to be eighteen, he said. You would go up to
Monterey for two weeks at a dollar a day, and after that
you would drill for an hour once a week for a year.

I said I was eighteen, but moving around, and
couldn't promise to meet once a week for a year to drill.

He said he'd fix it, and I went up to Monterey in a
uniform that night, and spent two weeks there, and
came back, and was standing on a corner in Los Angeles
waiting for the light to change when my father's younger
brother Mihran came by in his old Buick, with the top
down, and I shouted his name, and stepped in and sat
down.

Well, now, didn't I know my mother and my sisters
and my brother were looking for me?

He stopped at a telegraph office and sent my mother a
telegram.

And that was it, but in Monterey, on pass for an afternoon, in a pool room somewhere I heard a phonograph record of a song called *Valencia*, and it meant so much to me that I put it into a novel called *The Adventures of Wesley Jackson*. A couple of weeks ago I heard it again, sung in Spanish, on the radio, and a few days later I read in the Paris *Herald Tribune* that the man who had composed it had died, Pallida. I hadn't known he hadn't been dead long ago, but now that I knew, I felt bereaved.

Valencia had become a part of my life and fight, a part of all that I knew that nobody else knew.

15   The Stones

Well, now, isn't it interesting? Isn't it all lies, all distortion, all invention, all story-telling, all noble, all *with?* With the people, with *all* of the people, and not a word on behalf of stones.

I speak of stones because not long ago I was in Armenia, out past the high lake, Sevan, out where the little river, Arax, races among the stones, and suddenly each of the stones was a human being and very dear to me: faceless but true and proud as living human beings can never be proud, nameless, unknown, gathered together in hard silence. All with, and *again* with. Nothing *against.* What is it, with the Armenians, the Greeks, and the Jews? Are they the only people who have folk dances? They are not.

And the fact is the stones soon bored me. What could I do with them? I couldn't take them with me. I sat on one, I stood on one, I picked up a dozen that weren't too big to carry away, and I carried them away.

The Armenians who were born there looked at the stones and asked about them, and I said, "I want them. I want to have these stones."

They spoke of another place where the stones were better. They spoke of six or seven places where they were. They didn't get it, though.

"Boys, if I don't *see* the stones, if I don't look at them and see my family in them, the whole human race in them, they're *not* better, they're not *my* stones, they're not my human race."

One of the boys, an expert in the sayings of the people, said, *"Hayastan, karastan."*

Hayastan means the country of the Hais, pronounced Highs, the country of the Armenians, as they came to be inaccurately named: Ermeni, Armiansky, and there are surely three or four other versions of the inaccurate name, but among themselves they are Hais. And they ask the question, "Hayek?" "Are you a Hai?"

Karastan means the country of stones. Thus, the people and the stones, they are together, they are the same.

But that's not what I'm talking about. What I'm talking about is living, dying, and writing. Now, if I were required to write on stone, instead of on paper, what would I say? Hell, I'd *draw* it. I wouldn't say anything.

I'd put one of my drawings on a mountain bigger than Rushmore, with the foolish three heads making a shambles of a fine great hunk of pure rock: three heads that have been made to look like what people have agreed the three men looked like, but surely didn't.

But this isn't about my drawings, either. And the only time I saw the three heads on Rushmore was in a crime movie. There they were: my uncle Aram, my grandmother Lucy, and my cousin Hoosik, perfect likenesses of each of them, as large as life. Or almost, at any rate. Or Joe Gould, Joe Frisco, and good old Joe Nobody.

What is it with writers? What guts, what nerve, what presumption, what folly to imagine the stuff has got to get on paper, has got to get into print, has got to get onto a neatly designed page in a book, and out to the people, standing around in small disgruntled groups, waiting for it.

"What's the new word from you know who, what's his name, the kid, the old man, the drunk, the bum, the gambler, the killer, the wit, the cut-up?"

What fantasy to imagine even the man's own mother might find time to read, oh, maybe the first two or three pages, and then maybe the last half of the last page. "Very good, dear. And your father always thought you were useless. Keep trying. Some day you'll surely deserve a *Reader's Digest* Condensation." Old Mama knitting parachutes.

One thousand three hundred and six pages of small print, and the whole world dying to know what he's saying.

"What's he saying in this one?"

Well, there was the careful description of the country-side for two hours. A rabbit ran across a little of it, and then there was this summing up of the character of this sneak murderer—he had only a small amount of character, actually—and that took another hour. And then came the best part: talk, real natural talk—hours and hours of this talk, just as if it was you and me.

"Where was you?"

"Down the Senate saying the law. I didn't mean to be late. Was there something you wanted?"

"The money."

"How much this time?"

"I thought a dime."

"Another dime? Why not a nickel?"

"You can't get no real happiness out of a nickel any more, and you know I haven't been really, truly, deeply, zippy-like happy since the seventh child."

And then all of a sudden, no more talk—just a lot of great stuff about the history of shoes.

Did you know shoes were invented by a Chinese boy who wanted to make a hit with another man's wife, but of course they ate the first pair because he didn't know what he had invented.

And then three solid hours about feet, but not just human feet, animal feet, too.

What is it with writers? Can you blame the cheerful idiot who came upon Macaulay and said, "Always scribble, scribble, scribble, eh, Macaulay?" Whereupon of course Macaulay looked up and blushed, because wasn't it the truth, though?

All the same I like writers. I don't really know any, not as writers, at any rate. I know a few of them as themselves, I suppose, or at any rate as them public selves, for each of us to the other is the public, most likely. Isn't that interesting, too? With a little thought and care a hard-working writer could take an idea like that and write a piece for the series called *The Most Forgettable Character I Ever Met*. I forgot him. He may have died the following day, and now it's too late.

Or maybe a piece for the series called *The Little Misadventures of the Mind*.

This of course would be about a parrot who learned to think, but had a little trouble explaining the astonishing and useful mathematical discoveries it had made, and kept saying, "Leave your name and address, we'll send for you."

Why wouldn't I like writers? I'm a writer myself, even though I never make sense, and then all of a sudden something inspires me to make less. Old stones maybe. I don't know. The memory of them bugs me.

There are a million million stones in that little country, the whole country no bigger than a Texas ranch,
and every one of the stones is flesh and blood. The silent, faceless, raging stones of the Armenians, who actually aren't even Armenians, although they have never
been able to figure out how to make sense of that, because if they aren't Armenians, what are they? They are
stones, a nation of stones, they've got more dead than
they've got living, but the dead and the living are both
stones. They could never figure that out by themselves,
more than a million of them together in that little back-
yard of nowhere. What's his name's got to come along
and figure it out for them.

"Tell me, please, tell me, what nationality are the
English?" Stones.

"And the French?" Stones.

"And the Italians?" Stones.

"What nationality is the human race, then?"

Why, boys, the human race is Armenian, of course.
The alphabet proves it. Take only the first three letters
of it: *ipe, pen, kem.* If that isn't the human race, I don't
know what is. You'll see the three of them up there on
Rushmore any time you go to that crime movie.

"Hayek?"

And of course the answer is, *"Io."* What else?

Oh, I *know* there are four heads on Rushmore, don't
worry about that. It's just that even if the idea had
been right in the first place, which it wasn't, three
heads would have been enough.

16 The Thief

J. D. gave me back my job at the telegraph office after I had swiped a million tickets from the roll the manager of the Liberty Theatre had asked me in his third-floor office to present to the girl in the ticket-cage. What a stupid man. You don't give me a roll of tickets and expect me *not* to seize the bull by the horns, do you? And what disgrace, what humiliation, what the hell did you do a ridiculous thing like that for? Is it because you're thirteen years old now and trying to imitate adults? You've got to be more clever than *that* in your stealing. Steal the way that looks as if you're giving the hungry food, the thirsty water, and the mad comfort, the way the great men steal.

A life of crime in a lightning flash of time—zoop, and there in front of the great man, the troubled man, the astonished man, there in front of old J. D., thirty at the time, I suppose, a great hulking man, there stands the writer of this parable.

"Willie, the manager of the Liberty Theatre, Harry Slarp (Dirt and Doom? Is that what you said, J. D.? Is that his name?) just telephoned (What did he telephone for? What did he do that for?), and he told me something I can't believe. (Oh, you're going to *have* to believe it, J. D., and so am I. Christ, *how* I'm going to have to.) Willie, he said he gave you a roll of one thousand tickets and you took eleven of them, at a dime apiece. (That's a dollar ten, J. D.) I told him he must be mistaken, and if he isn't, there must be a perfectly sensible explanation. (You bet your life there is, J. D. I'm a thief. I'm a ten-cent movie-ticket thief.) I know you're not a thief, Willie. What happened?"

Well, there is always the flash of hope in the lie: *I didn't do it, it wasn't me, I don't know how the tickets got into my pocket, I'm no thief, I'm a Presbyterian, we pray at our house and do unto others as we would have others do unto us.*

There is always the same kind of flash that made the first flaw, and it is always eager to make the second, and after that—whoop, there goes another adult, clean-shaven, thoughtful (he's figuring what lamb to skin next), cheerful, encouraging to the sincere destitute—thrift and hard work are the secrets of success—and always neat and calm, haircuts every Saturday morning.

But I don't like haircuts that often.

I just couldn't go for the second flash and the second flaw.

It's not me, you know: it's Oliver Twist. I'm just writing it.

And soon now I will get to the words that were actually spoken, directly to a man I knew had believed in me: a man perhaps more nearly and truly myself than I was at that time: now hurt, six feet three, two hundred and twenty pounds, and raging, not against me but against the damned truth. Again and again, any man, any man in the world can be made a fool of in a flash by that unknowable something that trips the trigger of the weapon he is but means never to be.

Up until now my head had been down, away down,

on the other side of the world, in China. And the first thing I had to do was lift it all the way back up to the top of my neck and all the rest of me, and the damned thing was awfully heavy for a man weighing only a little over a hundred pounds. And then after the head was up I had to get behind the eyes, get entirely behind them, as if I had a right to be there, and then with all of myself there I had to look at J. D. and at the same time not give over to the sorrow I felt for him because he had believed in me and I had kicked his belief in the teeth.

And I did, and what I saw nearly made me decide on a life of crime, for the man was crying inside, the makings of a dozen tears were in each of his eyes, and his lips were moving on their own, because by now he knew, and a good thing I had let the flash to lie go by. I had *that,* at least.

I brought the tickets out of my pocket: "I thought there were *more* than eleven." By which I meant everything, that's all: shame, regret, arrogance, and the sorrow and sympathy of a fool for a great man.

He went to his desk and sat down. I went to my locker and removed the blue jacket of the Postal Telegraph Company, hung it up, and my cap, and hung it up. I shut the door of the locker and went back to his desk.

"I'll take the tickets back to him now."

I turned to go. His throat made a sound, but I didn't want to turn and look at him again.

"I'll give Henry your pay envelope," he said.

Well, now, old Dirt and Doom up there, he wasn't a child, like J. D. He was an adult.

"You ought to be sent to jail," old Dirt and Doom said.

Of course, there's no other solution to a great big fat problem like that, is there? And then all of a sudden the trigger tripped again, and this time it wasn't crime, it was either bawl or fight.

Well, fight, then.

"My job is to pick up and deliver telegrams. I'm not supposed to run free errands for you."

"You'll never work at that telegraph office again."

A man hears variations of that remark all his life.

A long *ah* of contempt, and then I was racing down the same stinking carpeted stairway that I had taken only fifteen minutes ago, before I had become a criminal, the lousy pipe organ still going with the lousy music of all the movies I had ever seen—well, movies are like that, you go racing down three flights of soft steps, the pipe organ is raising hell with the fantasy of high-style in the human experience, and you think you're in a movie yourself, you can do anything, so you roll off a few tickets and jam them into your pocket—"Oh boy, I can give them to the little kids in my neighborhood and tell them, 'Go ahead, see a cowboy movie for yourself, or a Bible one, or a kisser, Rudolph Valentino and Vilma Banky kissing, here, go to the Liberty Theatre free.' Why not? It's a big theatre."

Down one, two, three, and out, and there she is, the girl in the ticket cage, and *she* hates me, too. She glares at me.

"Caught you, didn't we? Caught you, caught you."

"Yes, ma'am, you caught me, you caught me redhanded. And here I go to join Roy Gardner—from now on none of this itty bitty stuff. From now on the banks, girlie, the big money. And no Jimmy Valentine stuff, either. No twiddling with the dials of safes. All straight rod work. The black gat, and then the money, or another banker drops dead."

I picked up my wheel and took one last look at the pretty little darling whose father was an adult, and I started racing down Van Ness as if I was on my way to the first stick-up.

I've written it. I've written it two or three times. The details are different every time. And it isn't that I'll get it right some day. It was always just right.

I got that kind of stuff out of the way right then and there.

And old Dirt and Doom *was* mistaken.

I was back in my blue coat and cap three days later, sent for by J. D. himself, who put it this way: "I did the same thing. You won't go there any more."

He meant I wouldn't go to the Liberty Theatre any more. But the world is small and time is swift and the world and time together are swift forgetters. I went to the Liberty Theatre, alone, a few days later, paid a dime, walked up to old Dirt and Doom's floor and office, so in case he came out he would see me, and then I took a seat in the gallery and listened to the lousy pipe organ crying about the children fast asleep in the burning house, and it was no good, the movie stank, so I went out to the water fountain and took a long drink, and hoped he'd step out and see me, but still he didn't, so I went down to the mezzanine and took a seat there, and the sleeping children were waking up and crying, a dog was barking, the first man who ever wore shoes was ducking under the fire and running into the house, and I didn't like it, it was too dark in there, and the music wasn't any better than the first time I heard it, so I went out again and had another drink, and there he was, standing just behind me, so I drank some more, and then some more, and then came up for air and turned and looked at him.

"Remember me, old Dirt and Doom? The criminal? I just paid a dime to see your lousy movie, but you can have it, you can have the dime and the movie both, and you'll always be the manager of this movie. You were born to it."

And out I went, and all I hope is that he never dies. Christ, J. D. died years ago—long, long ago. J. D. Tomlinson and don't ever forget it.

Well, wasn't J. D. *ever* no good, wasn't he ever wrong? Sure he was, but always with the earnestness, honor, and truth of a great man tormented by the damned failure everywhere, the damned smallness, not of things and ways alone, and not of others alone, but of himself. It murdered him to be this silly small thing whose only use was to run a crummy telegraph office. He'd sit and send a batch of telegrams, not stirring for three hours, and then click the key of the bug shut, get up, and moan, "Why?" Everybody in the office would look up at him, and he would shamble out of the office to the street, moving like a great bear, and after a few minutes he'd come back in and sit at his desk again.

The rocks I saw beside the racing river were the dead, but they were also the *living* who raced along like flowing water moaning, "Why?" And the rocks were in Armenia. Of course the human race is Armenian. How could it possibly be anything else? And nobody, nobody can be left out of the three who are carved in Rushmore. Old Dirt and Doom, lovey in the ticket cage, and the first man to wear shoes. The character to whom I was most forgettable was obliged at the water fountain to remember me. And the little misadventure of the mind that tripped me to the taking of the ten-cent tickets started a whole new series called *Ways to Truth*—whatever you do, don't take the soft stairs in the movie. Of course I like writers. It's just that I can't understand what they mean when it's all perfectly clear, unless it's the rabbit loping across part of the description.

And please don't imagine I'm not in earnest. It's just that I don't understand plot and went to Los Angeles when I wanted to go to San Francisco.

17   The School

The first ten years were really *years*, especially the first six, and of these six the first three were lost because the man didn't remember them, had to find out about them later, putting the pieces together.

And the second three were hard to work with because the man was neither little nor big, certainly not big enough, and not really at home where he was, although he *did* have the advantage of two sisters and a brother always near and could therefore suspect that he was *part* of a family, at any rate.

The seventh year wasn't too tough because his character was established and now all it was was a matter of time and movement. In due time he would leave that place and go to another place, his family's place, and he would begin another order of living: it might be another year, it might be two years, but it couldn't possibly be three, because Henry was nine, Zabe was twelve, and Cosette was fifteen.

It turned out to be less than a year, and the movement was south, by train, two hundred miles from Oakland to Fresno, back to the birthplace.

From seven to ten the years were pretty rough because there was this trouble about the matter of school: first, the matter of learning to read and write. Well, I thought

I'd never make it, but I won't belabor the point: I just couldn't get the hang of it, and everybody else could. Finally, though, I got it. All of a sudden it was all very simple. I could read, I could write, and I was awfully happy about it.

My handwriting was considered superior, perhaps the best in the whole school, and the things I wrote seemed to affect the teachers, some being opposed to the excessive length to which I went and the way I left the subject, and the ideas I had: let the rich take it easy about the poor, the poor might very well be *really* wealthier than the rich, let the proud watch it a little, they might have less to be proud of than they imagine, let the lucky few who happen to be truly superior share it with the others and not flaunt it.

The minute I knew how to write at all I had something to say, I had a sermon to give, I gave it, and some of the teachers considered this a kind of delinquency.

"Fifty words is all I wanted, on *How I Spent My Vacation,* not five hundred words on what you think is wrong with the people of Fresno."

A teacher named Miss Clifford. Well, with her it was quite simple: she hated me because I gave her a bad time by asking questions she couldn't answer.

Other teachers, however, especially, first, Miss Thompson, and then Miss Chamberlain, and finally Miss Carmichael, were affected differently.

Miss Thompson felt that she had discovered me, which I can't say she hadn't, although her discovery had little to do with me. I had been given an intelligence test before classes one morning, and she had been assigned to go over all of the tests. She was dumbfounded, thunderstruck, and aghast. She just had to see me immediately.

Thus, a messenger came to my class, handed a slip of paper to Miss Clifford, who ordered me to go with the messenger, a small Portuguese girl.

"What's she want?"

"You'll get it."

So what had I done this time?

Miss Thompson was studying my test when I went into her little room, adjoining the principal's office.

I recognized my writing and thought, "I guess I did something wrong and she'll make me take the test again."

"So you're William Saroyan?"

"Yes, Ma'am."

She was a rather large woman of about forty, who could be quite jolly and loud on occasion. She looked at me a moment without really looking at me, and then she said, "Well, there you are."

"Did I do something wrong?"

"Well, yes, I suppose, but not *really*. It's all right. You may return to your class now."

I went back to class, and that evening she came walking slowly up Van Ness Avenue on the Liberty Theatre side, across from my corner. My corner was the Fresno Republican Building, just across from the Rowell Building. It was one of the best corners in town. In order to be allowed to keep it I was expected to sell at least forty papers a day. I was hollering the headline and shoving the paper in front of people and saying, "Paper, Mister? Paper, Lady?" when Miss Thompson came along. She stood across the street and watched a moment, and then she came straight up to me and said, "William Saroyan," and walked away.

So she knew, did she? Well, good for her.

Miss Chamberlain, very handsome, very well made,

liked to throw ideas in my direction and see what I'd do with them, half-flirting, but of course I didn't know it at the time, and if I had, what good would it have done me? I liked her, but I didn't know anything about stuff like that. And then all of a sudden she took pleasure in punishing me by making me stand in the corner. Now and then she kept me after school, too, for nothing, really, and ordered me to work with her wiping the blackboards clean with a moist cloth, all the while keeping up a kind of running commentary about her job and the town and the kids she was trying to teach, the kids of immigrants, Armenians mainly, but others, too, a few Syrians, a few Assyrians, dark people with dark eyes you never could really understand. They kept to themselves, you never knew if you were getting through, they were still in another world, even though they were born in Fresno, and why did I encourage them to stay that way instead of opening up and being teachable, and *here,* instead of far away? Why did I set them a bad example by saying something in Armenian all of a sudden and making everybody laugh, embarrassing her? Didn't I know it was rude to speak a foreign language in class? How should she know what I was saying? Was I making fun of her? If so, why?

"No, we just like to talk Armenian once in a while, that's all."

"But why? This is America, now."

"The Americans don't like us, so we don't like them."

"So that's it. Which Americans don't like you?"

"All of them."

"Me?"

"Yes, you."

"How can you say that? I like or dislike people of all kinds on their own merits."

"Then, you don't think Armenians have any merits."

"Some do, and some don't."

"Sure, but *all* Americans are one hundred per cent perfect, aren't they?"

"You've got to stick together, don't you?"

"Don't *you? All* of you? Afraid of us? Our loud voices and swift ways? Don't you all stick together, too?"

"Well, maybe we do, but then, this *is* America, after all."

"But we're here, too, now, and if you can't stand the only way we can be Americans, too, we'll go right on being Armenians. Can I go, now? I'm late for my papers."

"Yes, you may go."

One day she said, "I'm leaving after this semester, to get married."

I felt glad she was going, because hadn't she kept me in after school again, keeping me from getting my papers on time and selling a few extra ones, making twenty or thirty cents extra? At the same time I wasn't glad I wouldn't be seeing her again. I felt that this was some kind of loss, but I hated school, I hated teachers, so why did I feel I was losing something? Well, obviously, because *she* felt she was, but I didn't look at it that way at the time. I was just glad she was going, and I was sorry she was going. We'd had some pretty good laughs together. She had said things I knew were intended for me alone, and a couple of times she had winked, or something like it, but I had never winked back. I didn't know how, and didn't think I should in any case. She was a pretty girl with a happy nature who found the going tough with so many sons and daughters of immigrants to teach. Twenty-two or twenty-three, most likely.

Best of all was Miss Carmichael, because she was both

beautiful and earnest, almost sorrowful, especially after she broke down one day and apologized to the class, explaining she had just heard that her brother had been killed in France. On the last day of school five minutes before the bell she asked me to please stay in my seat.

When we were alone she said, "This is not punishment."

She was seated at her desk. I was in the last seat in the last row, nearest the door, so I could always be the first out of the room and on my way to *The Evening Herald* Office and Press for my papers.

"I'm going up to San Francisco," she said, "and so of course I won't see you when school opens after summer vacation." She waited a moment, apparently trying to decide what to say next. "I want to thank you for your note when my brother was killed. But this is what I really want to tell you. I know about your family background, I've looked into it, I know there isn't a lot of money, but please don't let *anything* keep you from going to college. Will you remember that, always?" I nodded. "Good-by."

And I was out the door and on my way, but nothing doing, not me, the minute I could get out of school I was getting out. Why should I go to college? For more of that silly slow stuff? More of the insulting manners of the sons of the rich with their fine clothes and their everlastingly new and polished shoes? Let *them* go to college. They needed it. I didn't.

There is a school somewhere near Bitlis, in Armenia, called Mount Holyoke, for girls—or rather there *was* such a school—and I sometimes heard it referred to by my mother and by her sisters and by my grandmother Lucy, all of whom pronounced it Montolyo. Now, none of these women had ever gone to that rather high-falut-

ing school, opened and operated by American Protestant
missionaries. They hadn't gone to any school at all.
Neither of my grandmothers knew how to read and
write, and both were famous for their intelligence, and
Lucy for *more* than intelligence—for insight, for wit,
and when necessary for parody and sarcasm of a high
order. She gave names to people that stayed with them
for life, and the names were apt, if almost always unkind—but that's all right, the names were always given
to the vain, the pompous, the dishonest, the pretentious,
the stupid, the crude, and the cruel. Whenever she gave
a name to ignorant people who were decent, it was a
name that never offended them, and in fact pleased
them.

One day I heard Lucy say of somebody, "Of course
she was educated at Montolyo. Being stupid, it was both
urgent and necessary."

No college for me. All the same I had been deeply
moved by Miss Carmichael's farewell message, by her
earnestness, the tone of her voice, and the profound sorrow she carried around with her, which I felt was related to the sorrow I carried around with me always, in
spite of my compulsion to cut up, to break the monot-
ony, to make the kids laugh.

Of course it was a great time. It stank.

18   The Nose

A few months after I was ten, in 1918, the war ended, the dead were counted, and the lies were weighed and measured. It was time now for new and different lies, and it was no trouble at all for anybody, but it wasn't easy to sell papers any more, because the real excitement was all over for a while. The news simmered down to the little routine lies that don't impel people to buy a paper.

The years from 1918 to 1928, to my arrival in New York, were rough, tough, desperate, difficult, lonely, luminous, wonder-charged, and dangerous, for I was there now entirely and fully, a man with his sex upon him, pushing him to woman, while the rest of him which had been pushing to art went right on pushing, too.

I had no way worth speaking of with girls. They meant too much for me to be at ease with them. I either wanted them wholesale, so to say, or I wanted the one with whom I meant to make a new and full life of truth, beauty, honor, art, and six or seven other high-class things. A family, or a whole new human race: her kids by way of me. But I didn't see her anywhere, and if I did, or thought I did, she was going somewhere, and I didn't know her in any case.

But I *saw* girls everywhere, and weren't they real crazy, though? Weren't they loaded with the stuff I could never stop wanting and could never get, too, because I wanted it so badly my wanting made me clumsy and quick and wrong and ashamed? And look at the guys in the movies. Look at how they went about it: the deep chuckling throaty voice and lip-smacking confidence of Clark Gable, for instance, saying, "Baby, I know just what's the matter with you—it's *me*, and I'm here to settle the matter, just as soon as you stop trying to be a tiger and become the nice little purring kitten you *really* are."

But I won't really try to approximate the styles of movie sex talk, or try to sum up all of the sex techniques of all of the famous movie heroes.

My own technique will be enough, most likely.

I took an Armenian girl to a movie in Fresno when I was seventeen and she was fifteen, because she had a gay reputation among the boys, and so after the movie, walking her home, passing through the Court House Park, and feeling pretty lumpy and romantic and scared, I stopped and tried to kiss her, but she giggled and said, "Oh, no, no, you mustn't, please, my mother would kill me."

Her mother would kill her for *what?* What had I done? All I wanted to do was hold her, and then see about kissing her. There was a way of getting my nose around her nose without bumping and hurting them. I had watched the experts in the movies, taking it slow and easy, and I had especially made a point of noticing the way the noses were made to fit gracefully, especially Barrymore's, with his nostrils flaring like the nostrils of an excited horse. I hadn't done *anything* yet, and already she was yelling about Mama.

"Oh, no, no, you mustn't, please, my mother would kill me."

Well, now, what was the answer to *that?* What would Clark Gable say in a similar situation? I couldn't think of anything Gable might say, or anything especially apt, either, and I kept wondering about her mother, a woman I had never met, so I said, "What's your mother's name?"

"Rose," the girl said. "Vartouhi in Armenian."

"That's a nice name." Well, now, where was the *moon,* at any rate, for God's sake? Maybe I could bring in the moon and put it to work.

I took her hand gently and was pleased that she didn't draw it away. Maybe I'd do all right, after all.

"Look, Diana. The moon."

She looked.

"That's not the moon. That's the big light they keep on all night just outside the County Jail."

Well, she was right, and so of course I felt a little silly, but at the same time I couldn't help being curious about the light.

"Why do they leave it on all night?"

"To prevent escapes, of course," the girl said.

"To make attempted escapes *visible* is what you mean, isn't it?"

"Yes, of course. If it's dark and they escape, nobody'll see 'em."

"If it's light and nobody's around, nobody'll see 'em, either. Nobody's around now except us and it's not even eleven yet. There must be some other reason why they keep the light on all night."

Well, even I knew this wasn't it at all.

She began to walk, so I tried to draw her back, but she began to tug.

"No, I've got to get home. My mother'll kill me."

I decided I had better grab her and hold her, and then see if I could manage the business of the noses. When I had her, I tilted my head to one side and began to move my lonely soul towards her pretty eyes and nose and mouth, and for an instant it looked as if I had made it, but suddenly she began to wag her head from side to side, so that if I had gone on in with my soul I would have hurt my nose.

I wondered if it might not be possible to get with the rhythm of the wagging, and in that way get my nose safely in place, stop the wagging, and start the kissing.

I timed the action and was all set to try it when she said, "Well, then, why *do* they keep the light on all night?"

"Graft. Somebody at the Pacific Gas and Electric made a deal with somebody in the Department of Parks and Playgrounds."

She stopped wagging, to listen, and I believed my chance had come, so I moved in quickly. She lifted her head and caught the side of my nose with her chin. There was a cracking sound, and I drew away. The girl ran as fast as she could go, about fifty yards, I suppose, and then stopped.

Was my nose bleeding? Was I supposed to run after her, or what?

Yes, my nose was bleeding, and no, I'd be damned if I would run after her, no matter what the rules might be. I walked.

When I reached her she said, "Is your nose bleeding?"

"Yes, it is."

"I'm sorry. I really didn't mean to give you a bloody nose."

"That's all right. It'll stop in a minute. What did you run away for?"

"Well, you're crazy. You can't just take a girl to a movie and then expect to kiss her and hold her and fool around and make her lie down and force yourself upon her and all that stuff."

Was she giving me instructions, or what, because if she was, I'd try to follow them the minute my nose stopped bleeding.

"Hold your head back," she said. "My, you've got red blood. I don't think I've ever seen such red blood. Thick, too. Has it stopped?"

"I think so."

I sniffed a couple of times, blew my nose softly with a part of my handkerchief that wasn't already bloody, there was no blood, so I folded the handkerchief and put it in the back pocket of my trousers. And then I reached for her hand again.

"Oh, no, you don't," she said. "I would have run all the way home, but I'm afraid of crazy men hiding in these parks."

"What do you mean, crazy?"

She had drawn away, out of reach, and was ready to break into a trot again.

Well, does she want me to chase her, or what?

I lunged for her, because it seemed to me I ought to do whatever she had been accustomed to having done, and she broke and ran.

I decided to run after her, but not really as swiftly as I could if I wanted to, just enough to give her the pleasure or whatever it was of being run after, but suddenly she screamed, and it was as good as anything I had ever heard in a zombie movie. For a moment I believed

it might be somebody else in the park, but it wasn't.
The minute she screamed, though, I stopped running,
and so did she. I approached her cautiously, because
there was no telling what she might do next.

"What did you do that for?"

"You scared me, running that way."

"Why?"

"I'm not a fast runner, I always get caught, and it
always makes me scream."

More documentation?

"Well, you'd better not scream any more. You'll wake
up the guys in the County Jail."

What had the other boys done, who had given her
her great reputation, and had spread it all over town?
I had already used up the better part of a dollar taking
her to a movie and buying her an ice cream soda, and
all I'd gotten for it so far was a bloody nose, a small track
meet, and a loud long scream. Maybe they had *asked*
her in a nice way.

Well, hell, I couldn't do *that*. I *wouldn't*.

I walked her home, pretty much in silence. We went
up on the front porch and she sat down in the rocking
chair.

"Well, good night, then."

"Don't go," she said. "Sit down and let's talk."

Talk? What could we possibly talk about?

"What do you want to talk about?"

"You. I hear you're a writer. What do you write?"

Oh, no.

"Well, stories, I guess."

"*Secret* stories?"

"Well, I guess you could call them secret stories if
you wanted to. They've never been printed, I mean."

"Why not? You could make a lot of money putting stories in books."

Her mother called out from the parlor: "Manoushak?"

"Yes, Mama, I'm home, it's all right."

No more from Mama.

"Manoushak?" I said. "That means Violet, doesn't it? Where's the Diana from?"

"I don't like Manoushak. It isn't modern."

"Oh. Well, I guess I'll get on home."

"No, don't go. Tell me about writing. I always wanted to meet a writer. How do you get your ideas?"

After about an hour of this, her mother came out on the porch. She was a dumpy little woman in her late thirties, I suppose, all rouged up, and smoking a cigarette. She looked me up and down, and then ordered her daughter into the house.

Then, she looked me up and down again, and said, "Who are you? What do you want with my daughter?"

"Nobody. I took her to a movie, that's all."

"Why? Why do you want to take my daughter to a movie?"

"She likes movies."

"She has seen many movies. Why did you take her?"

"Well, if you didn't want me to take her, I'm sorry. Good night."

"Just a minute," the mother said. All in Armenian of course. "How old are you?"

What was this, now? Had I gotten the reputations mixed up, or what?

"I'm seventeen." And then for some crazy reason I said, "How old are *you?*"

The woman smiled and took a big drag on her cigarette.

"Over twenty-one," she said in English, which for
her appeared to be the language of sin, so to say. "Do
you smoke cigarettes?"

"Now and then."

She held out her pack: Obaks. I took one and lighted
it, and she said, "We live alone here, my daughter and
I. She has her own room and I have mine. Would you
like to come in for a minute? After my daughter is in
bed and asleep? A mother has to be very careful about
her daughter."

"Yes, I suppose she does."

"My daughter is so inexperienced, so inexperienced.
A boy can learn things from older people. But a girl
can't. That's why I have to be so careful. What is your
name?"

I told her, and she said, "My name is Rose. You seem
nervous. You mustn't be nervous. Do you like my—
house?"

"Well, yes, I think it's a very nice house."

"It's much nicer inside."

You bet, and she was loaded with some kind of per-
fume that was scaring me to death.

A man and woman walked by on the sidewalk and
looked up at the two of us standing there, and I only
wished they weren't Armenians, and if they were, I only
wished they didn't know her, and didn't know me, because this mother and this daughter were really old-
fashioned, and I didn't want to give them a bad name
in any way.

When she believed her daughter was sound asleep—
after not much more than five minutes—I thanked her

for the cigarette and a pleasant chat, and then hurried down the stairs and up the street.

When I first heard the alley cats at sex around the house on San Benito Avenue I believed it was little children involved in some sort of unholy torture, the precise nature of which I couldn't even imagine. A voice is a voice, a cry is a cry, and as far as I knew cats only drank milk, caught mice, purred, and meowed. Poor little kids, poor little kids, I thought, wondering who they were.

They were everybody.

19   The Whistler

I whistled a lot, almost from the first day at the orphanage, even though at that time I didn't even know *how* to whistle. I could make a kind of hissing sound in trying to learn, though. Soon, I *had* learned, and I whistled all the time, even among people. I was away out there, alone, even when I was among people, and they didn't like it, they considered it rudeness, as of course it might have been had I known there could be any such thing for me. I certainly had never meant to be rude.

The people are busy talking, I don't know what it's all about, I can't understand them, and so I'm whistling.

I'm whistling at the orphanage, and Blanche Fulton who has come there voluntarily to look after the smaller kids at her own expense is trying to teach us something about art. She's bought paper and paints and crayons and pencils and pens and ink, and she's really not a bad sort at all, but my whistling bothers her. I've got a big sheet of white paper, I've taken a big brush, I've smeared it around in watery red paint and I've sloshed it this way and that on the paper, steadily whistling *I Love You, California. You're the greatest state of all. I love you in the winter, summer, spring, and in the fall. I love your rugged mountains, your dear oceans I adore.* And there goes some very black black around the red stuff, and it's beginning to look like something, although not like anything anybody else has ever seen, because it was all mine, which I was making right then and there out of this crazy love of California and its dear oceans.

"William, please don't whistle that way. It disturbs the others."

I stop, because when you're that little every order you hear is automatically obeyed immediately, but by the time I was sloshing a very bright green among the red and black I was also going great with *I love you* again.

"William."

I stopped again. I walked to where the window looked out at the green hill, and I saw a bird out there hopping around, pecking at little things, and eating them. Now, that was very interesting, that little thing out there, and so *I love you in the winter.*

"William." The voice loud now and unhappy, a little astonished.

I stop again. Well, it's a big place, you know, but what they've got is a lot of everything, most of it *too* big, a little oversize, like the water away down the hill, far away, one of the dear oceans, most likely. Fall in *there,* and there you'd be, and no damned place to stand, just all that water. No good. *Your dear oceans I adore.* Life is great, even at the Fred Finch Orphanage, even in spite of matrons giving you a bath once a week, strange women with red noses and red hands lifting you up and dropping you down in the tub and scrubbing you. It was insulting, but it wasn't half as bad as being out there in all that water of the dear ocean with no place to stand. *I love you, California.*

"William, will you please stop whistling and go back to your picture?"

I stop, I go back.

We used to gather together in age groups on Sunday morning and march to Sunday School, where we sang, *Joy to the world, the Lord has come.* Well, whoever it was, and there was no indication that it wasn't in fact me, it seemed right enough to put it that way: joy to the world, here I am at last. Hadn't we had boiled duck eggs for breakfast, as we almost always did on Sundays? Duck eggs are bigger. They taste better, too. They are good to see in their brown shells before you break them to get the white and yellow out, hot and smelling good.

Well, now the singing at Sunday School is over and somebody has taken it upon himself to make a speech direct to God. He is going along in the usual way and it sounds pretty big, but all I know is *joy to the world, here I am.*

After the amen, the professional man says, "Who was the boy who whistled all during the prayer?"

"Yes," I think, "who *was* that? Got to let the man speak to God without somebody whistling all the time."

Quite a fuss is made trying to find out who it was. This boy and then that boy is saying, "No, sir, it wasn't me. No, sir, I didn't whistle."

And so finally the matter is dropped, the subject is changed, and an hour or more later, marching back to the orphanage, I suddenly remember.

"Croak, *I* was the one who whistled. I whistled the whole time he prayed, but I didn't even know I was whistling."

One summer night they made a great big fire and everybody in the whole orphanage, boys and girls together, sat around the fire and sang *Tenting Tonight.* I didn't even know what tenting was. I thought it must be a kind of half-sorrowful, half-joyous giving over to memory, old memory, the oldest, far back in time. *Many are the hearts that are weary tonight, tenting on the old camp ground.* Well, later I found out it was a Civil War song, but whether for the North or for the South I still don't know, and why *we* were singing it I don't know, either, unless it was such a beautiful song, one of the best I had ever heard certainly, or because we ourselves were up late that way, with a great fire lighting up our faces and making us warm all over.

And then we moved along to a Mexican song, or perhaps it was Spanish, it doesn't matter, what matters was that it was about this girl Juanita, who stole my soul, who was the loveliest creature that ever breathed. Just to hear about her made you rejoice and almost weep, because somehow, call it fate or call it what you will, she is yours, she belongs to you, she knows you from the beginning, loves you, lives for you, breathes for you, precisely as you love, live, and breathe for her.

And then we sang a song of trouble, about a quarrel so unfortunate that it brought tears to my eyes and a lump to my throat: *I don't want to play in your yard, I don't like you any more. You'll be sorry when you see me sliding down our cellar door.*

And one day Blanche Fulton took us by ferry across the bay to the San Francisco Fair, in 1915. *The Panama-Pacific International Exhibition* or whatever it was officially called. A man named Art Smith was flying an airplane around where everybody could see it, and he was doing something called *the loop-the-loop*, turning the flying thing over and over. This was big, new, and special, and not just the airplane, the whole place.

We saw the whole Fair, including two camels following two Arabs in their native costumes.

We heard a band, too, a whole great big military

band, and somebody kept speaking about Sousa, and
Sousa's Band, and the great marches that Sousa had written, like the one we had just heard: *And the monkey
wrapped his tail around the flagpole.*

There *were* these interesting things.

Then came Fresno, home, family, and difference.

Somebody somewhere had a phonograph, and he put
on a record that wasn't American, it was Armenian. It
was different. Even so, wasn't it mine even more than
any other song I had ever heard or had ever whistled?
Wasn't it more *deeply* mine? It *seemed* to be. *Well,
walk, walk, walk, wounded homeless, unkillable homeless, well, walk, walk, walk, walk.*

"What is this?"

"This is *us*," somebody said. "This is ours, this is one
of our songs, this is from our country."

I whistled it all the time.

Weren't we all walking that way and losing one another and dying?

And then somebody put on another song, the like of
which I had never before heard. It was something like
the first one, but not quite, not really. This one was
mine, too, but different, and somebody said, "Kurdish,
it's a song of our Kurds, the Kurds of Bitlis."

Fire, fire, fire, fire, fire. Meaning love, the voice of the
man high, the voice of the woman higher, the word for
fire soft and swift: *nari, nari,* the other words guttural,
from the throat, from deep back inside the whole man.

I liked it, wanted it, and got it right then and there.

And then somebody put on another song, and again
it was mine, it was related to the other two, but it was
different, too: and somebody said Turkish.

The singing was so sorrow-laden sometimes the singer
had to stop—cold. And then start again.

But weren't the Turks our enemies? Of course they were, but this was something that was ours just the same, and I liked it and got it and kept it. *Ahkh, yavroum, the singing of the nightingale tells me of home, and I cry for the brook where I drank our cold water.*

And then came the War, and God knows you know the songs we lived by if we lived at all in those days, if you were up and about then: *It's a Long Way to Tipperary. When It's Apple-blossom Time in Normandy. Just a Baby's Prayer at Twilight. K-K-K-Katy. Oh, What a Pal Was Mary. There's a Long, Long Trail A-winding, into the Land of My Dreams.*

How Ya Gonna Keep 'em Down on the Farm, After They've Seen Paree? I'm Forever Blowing Bubbles. Sailing Down the Bay to Tripoli.

And the hell with them. I whistled them all.

20   The Madman

If there is turning, if there are points, if there is a turning point in anybody's life, if turnings are constant and
points endless, what may I presume to have been the
turning point of my life?

It was my birth.

From then on I had it made.

There was no other turning after that.

If birth was the only turn and a turn to the right, the
next turn has got to be death and a turn to the left. And
that will have been it, that will have been who he was,
and how he did. Saroyan and tried.

In my childhood the numbers one to nine took on
an importance for me that had little to do with reason,
although the importance had something to do with
meaning, with a kind of personal, if not secret, meaning.
Zero, however, meant nothing. Perhaps it was a trick,
although it had great beauty.

Even though I was born in 1908, the number 8 was
not my favorite. It was 7, and there was no accounting
for this. From somewhere and by some means it had
come to me that my number was 7, and of course I was
devoted to it.

You might imagine the value of 7 should have been

quite clear to me, since my real beginning had been during the year 1907, late in November or early in December, allowing the usual nine months for the interior formation of a body and its thrust from the interior to the exterior. But my connection with 7 was not based upon the animal embrace of male and female, mother and father, in the accidental formation of a new person. I simply noticed that of all of the numbers I knew, I preferred 7, I believed it was my own, I cherished it. I felt a kinship with it. I have said accidental formation of a person, in this case a person which was given the name I go by, because sometimes when the male and female embrace a life starts and sometimes a life doesn't.

There is an interval of three years between the births of the children of my father and mother, and surely during those intervals there was more than one embrace, for my father loved my mother. From her own talk, overheard, I gathered that she was not crazy about the procreative act, so to put it, by which I do not mean that she was without love, emotion, or passion. Quite the contrary, I should imagine. It was just that the act did not mean for her what it meant for my father. I gathered that he was inclined to move in that direction frequently and that she was not invariably eager to join him in the same spirit. All the same, it must be presumed that there were many cleavages that did not result in the beginning of a new person, and since there was no indication of any order of knowledge by which to avoid, by which to prevent, or to seek to prevent, such a beginning, every actual beginning must be considered to have been accidental. Still, the time-spacing between the four beginnings has an unmistakable regularity, which suggests that there *might* have been a method of control, but what the method was I cannot guess. I must presume the regularity was accidental.

Now, if your people tend to have and to cherish great numbers of children, from six to twelve, for instance, and if there is an interval of three years between the birth of each new member in your own family, it must be presumed that there is an expectancy of a long life for both the female and the male, for the mother and the father, the agents of the process, acting on behalf of the animal order by which forms of life are perpetuated, maintained, extended, and given variations.

If the characteristics of persons in any given line are genetically valid for six generations on both sides of the line, male and female, the apportioning of these characteristics equally, if there might be said to be an equitable distribution of them, would require twelve new lives for each family.

Each new life in every family is certainly in many ways unlike each of the other new lives in the family, even while a certain constant is maintained in all of them.

In my family this constant may be said to have been what I have come to call the Saroyan Scowl. This may not be a very accurate description, but at the same time, it will do. It is not by any means the only constant, but it seems to me that it is the dominant one. I will speak of it again, most likely, because it has a bearing on the matter of the writer's identity and the thoughts and acts of his life.

It was early said of the fourth child and second son of Armenak and Takoohi Saroyan that he was the inheritor of the nature and spirit of a man called *Bent Baro,* which is the Armenian way of saying Mad Baro, whose proper name was Barunak Saroyan. He was the brother or first cousin of my mother's father, hence a Saroyan by birth, rather than by adoption.

What was he? What was his trade or profession? Well, as far as I was able to gather he was mainly a cut-up. He was said to have been as strong as a bull, and was famous for the heavy things he could lift and carry, although his trade was not that of the *hamal*, the man who earns his living by lifting and carrying. He was a big man, he was hearty, he was loud, he was outspoken to the point of vulgarity. He was impatient with all of the members of his immediate family, and he would fly into a rage if his wishes weren't instantly granted, frequently even when he had not made them known. He expected his wife and children to be able to know from a glance that he wanted silence, for instance. I gather that he would have been born in Bitlis in the late 1840's or early 1850's, about sixty years before my birth.

What about his own children? They are gone, they are dispersed, they did not leave Bitlis when the direction taken by many of the Saroyans was West, to America. They appear to have perished in the various religious, political, and economic flare-ups between the Turks and the Armenians. Some of his sons and daughters *may* have survived, and they may have married and raised families, but there is no knowledge of this, as of course there does not need to be. As small children, some of the boys and girls may have become lost, and these boys and girls may have been taken in by Turks or Kurds, Arabs or Persians, and they may have become members of new families. They may have married others than Armenians, and they may have raised large families, never knowing they were in fact Saroyans, the sons and daughters of Mad Baro. This sort of thing happens all the time, not only in that troubled part of the world, but in all parts of it. And it doesn't matter too much one way or the other.

But the fact that a man or a woman had been fathered by Barunak did not necessarily mean that they were very much like him.

And Lucy, soon after I became established in the family after the years at the orphanage, remarked again and again, "He is Mad Baro all over again."

I heard the remark and presumed the connection was not far-fetched, for my mother did not deny it, or protest against it, but remembered Barunak, glanced at me, and became thoughtful, or angry all over again if the occasion for Lucy's observation had been behavior which had been poor.

Now, when I was in Armenia not long ago I visited the home in Erivan of a famous Armenian poet. This home had been made into a kind of museum. The poet had fathered eleven children before he was forty, even though he spent most of his time on the town. One morning he went home when everybody else was getting up and going to work. His wife complained that he did not come home very often. "I came home eleven times, didn't I?" the poet said.

In any case, like it or not, the theory was that it had come to me to preserve and extend the qualities of this man Barunak Saroyan. This jokester, prankster, upstart, cut-up, loud-mouth, and hooligan, who was irritable, short-tempered, unreasonable, demanding, and surely at least a little mad. He certainly refused to join the other branches of the family in picking up and moving to America. When the great national hero, Kerop of Bitlis, whom the Turks had hunted for years, had been betrayed and finally captured by the Turks, Barunak, in the middle of the night, went from one Saroyan house to another, pounding on roof doors and loudly calling out to the men of every family by name, saying, "Get up, they've beheaded Kerop. They've stuck his head upon a spear for all to see." That's as far as the story I overheard goes, but the implication is that he organized the Saroyans and other Armenians for retaliatory action, which of course in turn meant Turkish retaliatory action, back and forth, and which may account for the apparent disappearance of Mad Baro's line.

I neither liked nor disliked my connection with the man, but I was devoted to my connection with 7. This sort of number-and-person relationship is probably universal, or at any rate it is probably true that at some time or other people in general associate themselves with one or another of a variety of numbers, signs, objects, forms, ideas, in a manner that must be considered both meaningless and mystical, and without *ever* reaching a decision about which it is most: meaningless, that is, or with an unknown meaning. A whole nation associates itself, to go a little further, with the sun, as the Japanese do, or at any rate have done. Or with a quarter moon and a star, as the Turks do, or have done. Or with a mountain, Ararat, as the Armenians do, or have done. But these are not the most apt of illustrations, most likely. And it doesn't matter, because that which *does* matter (a little) is that associations of one sort or another are inevitable.

There is simply a great deal to be associated with, and there is a constant association with All, known or not.

After a time, however, 7 ceased to be my number.

When I was ten or eleven 9 became my number, and a few years later 3 became my number.

But after I was twenty or twenty-one there was a

steady inner movement (and gradual awareness of it) toward the number 8. This seemed to make at least a little sense, because I began in the year 1908. And the years thereafter in which 8 was the last of the four numbers, 1918, 1928, 1938, and so on, were years of special interest to me, for with the arrival of each I had had ten more years of time upon myself.

21   The Wanderer

The years 1928 to 1938 were great years for me, but perhaps they weren't, and I want to look into this. Now, when the fellow wrote the book of Ecclesiastes, he repudiated his whole life, but it is necessary to notice that he wrote as an old man, a different man, a tired man, a wiser man perhaps, but surely only *differently* wise, for he must have been wise in his youth, too, and in his middle years as well. All was *not* vanity until he *said* it was.

In short, it is possible for any man to make a decision about the past any time he feels like it. He can say it was great, or he can say it was lousy, and while each may be true, the truest thing of all by that time is the man himself or what's left of him, and *why* he is saying what he is saying. The fellow who wrote that great book of the Old Testament appears to have said what he said because he was old now and wasn't equal to the grand fun of his youth and middle years. His wisdom was fairly useless to anybody excepting an old man.

Early in 1929, before the end of January, I was back in California after about five months in New York. I went back by chair car because it was all I could afford, and it was a good long, slow ride. I had failed again, for in my heart I had gone in the expectation of staying

gone. Or at any rate until I might have gone back as a
visitor, a man of fame and fortune. But I had gotten
sick, and then I had gotten *home*sick, and I had gone
back pretty much the same as I had been when I had
left. Nothing and nobody. At any rate, the eventual out-
come was still unknown, and time was running out.

Would I make it, or was I dreaming? Was I being a
fool? Why was it in fact *necessary* to *insist* I was somebody and that I had something to do? Something other
than find a job, earn wages, take a wife, bring up a family? Nobody else in my world was going to so much
trouble about the matter. Why was I? All of my friends
were quite willing to mosey along with themselves and
the world in a manner so ordinary and so undemanding
as to seem to me entirely meaningless. I couldn't understand it. Why weren't they restless? Why were they satisfied simply to be there and to let it go at that? Was it
possible that *they* were actually wise and I foolish? We
were all over twenty now. Everybody I had known from
the age of eight was anywhere from twenty to thirty,
and everybody was perfectly at home where he was, so
why wasn't I, too?

Well, first of all, just where was my home? Was it
Fresno, where I was born? Was it San Jose, where my
father died? Was it Oakland, where I spent four very
important years? Was it San Francisco, where the whole
family had moved, where my father had lived for a number of months in 1911, where my mother had lived when
her kids had been at the orphanage across the bay, where
I had once lived with her for two or three months, in
a furnished room on Laguna Street, and had gone to
school nearby, and then had gone back to the orphanage? Was it New York, where my father had lived from
1905 to 1908, working and studying and sometimes

preaching, to earn money to send to my mother, so she could bring the three kids to New York, too? Was it Bitlis? Was it London, which for some reason I loved? Was it a place I hadn't visited yet? Or was it the whole world? Or nowhere?

Well, I didn't know, although I suspected it was not quite a matter of that kind at all.

Home was in myself, and I wasn't there, that's all. I was far from home.

But hadn't I gotten homesick for the first time in my life while I had been in New York, during Christmas week of the year 1928? I had. Well, what had I longed for during that homesickness? The rented house on San Benito Avenue that I remembered so vividly? Our own house, bought with our own savings, at 3204 El Monte Way in Fresno, in which I had grown so swiftly, from which I had gone off on my own for the first time? Was it the third-floor flat at 2378 Sutter Street in San Francisco from which I had taken a bus to New York?

Well, perhaps it was a little of each of the places where we had lived, but it was probably something else, too. It was probably us, a family, a continuous and difficult if not frequently impossible state of being together, all of us in the same place. The food and the sitting together to eat it, or more frequently sitting to eat it whenever one or another of us got home from work, or got up in the morning, some earlier than others. The rooms where our tables and chairs were. The beds, the order of coverings we slept under: wool from the old country, beaten until light, and sewed into thick blankets. Who understands home? Who understands himself?

22 The Visit

One day in September of 1928 I looked into the telephone directory and found that the widow of the man after whom my father had named me lived in Brooklyn, and so I took the subway to the nearest station and went to the house and rang the doorbell.

When she opened the door, the widow of Dr. William Stonehill said, "You are Armenak Saroyan's son. Please come in."

I was astonished that she knew, and for a moment I wondered *how* she knew, since she had never seen me. I was twenty years old, my father had been dead seventeen years, she hadn't seen him in twenty years, I hadn't telephoned to ask if I might pay her a visit. The fact is that when I had taken the subway to Brooklyn I had believed I only wanted to *see* where she lived, but then suddenly, for some reason, I believed I ought to press the button of the doorbell. Perhaps she wouldn't be at home at four in the afternoon.

I had seen a photograph of her with her husband and my father since I had been eight years old. She was a tall, handsome woman of thirty-five or so in the photograph, and she was precisely the same woman when she opened the door.

Well, why had I gone out there? Was that part of the

search for a home, a world, a way? Her house was a kind of instantly recognizable self-portrait: handsome, orderly, slightly severe, but at the same time warm.

She was being visited by a friend, not unlike herself, somebody in church work. They prepared tea, and we sat and drank the tea and ate little cakes and talked.

This woman knew my father before I was born, and she knew my mother, and my mother's mother, but I gathered that she had been a little let down by the women, because neither of them had cared very much for her good works, and were entirely unwilling to accept and wear the corsets she had given them. They hadn't been at home in the correct atmosphere she and her husband maintained, and they may even have been a little scornful of it. And until their arrival in New York my father had been entirely at home in that atmosphere and with them, and they had always imagined that he intended to continue in the ministry in New York, as she put it, or in nearby Paterson, where he had given sermons in English and in Armenian.

But soon after the arrival of Takoohi and Lucy, she said, my father became deeply troubled, for they wanted him to drop everything, a whole career that promised to be brilliant, and move to California. They simply did not want to live in New York, or for that matter in New Jersey, or anywhere else in the East. They wanted to go to California because so many others said the life there was not unlike the life they had known in Bitlis.

And so at last my father had given in to them, and they had all gone along to California. Soon afterwards her husband had been called to a better life and world, and a few years later so had Armenak, and so on.

Well, it was informative, but it was depressing, too. Somewhere during the tea and conversation she said

that in working among the Armenian immigrants she
and her husband had received notes from many of them
but hadn't heard from them again. This puzzled me.
What sort of notes had the Armenian immigrants written? Did *all* Armenians write and hand what they wrote
to people who helped them? I imagined the notes as
having been in a kind of basic but inadequate English:
"Me, Vahan Muggerditchian of Bitlis, embrace Dr. William Stonehill and wife for great help in New York."
And so on. But I wasn't sure I had got the thing right.
I waited for clarification, and tried to make known by
the silent ways we have in such circumstances that I
would like to hear more about this matter. I was aware
that the lady knew I was puzzled, but still she did not
tell me anything more. At last I felt I must simply ask.

"I don't believe I understand about the notes they
gave you. What sort of notes were they?"

Well, this was a matter that had apparently always dis-
mayed her, and she showed it now.

"Why, they were notes for the loans my husband and
I made to them. They all promised to repay the loans
but not one of them did. Not one of them."

And now I was angry. What the devil was the matter
with the Armenians? How could they accept money
from such kind, gentle, refined, earnest and helpful people, and hand them notes, and not pay them back? And
of course I felt deeply ashamed and embarrassed.

"Did my father or mother or grandmother hand you
a note?"

If they had I meant to pay it in full, with interest, as
soon as possible. But the lady said my father and mother
and my grandmother had paid their own way entirely.
They had worked for wages, and when they had saved
enough for railroad tickets they had gone to California.

23   The Eaters

Eddie Jabulian was a messenger at Postal Telegraph
after having shined shoes at an alley stand for a year
after graduating from high school. Eddie was nineteen
to my fourteen, but he learned telegraphy, and after the
telegraph companies brought in teletype machines, Eddie got work in little railroad depots.

He used to come in from a long delivery and say,
"Here, let me show you what I had."

And he would smooth out the wrapper of a nickel
candy bar with a name like Golden Jubilee, or Forever
Yours, or Jungle Jive. What he meant was that he had
eaten. This would always be at night, when we worked
the night shift, from four to one.

One time he came in but didn't ask me to see what he
had had, so I said, "Eddie, didn't you have anything on
this long delivery?"

"I had something all right, don't worry about me, I
take good care of myself, candy for quick energy, but I
know you, I been watching you out of the corner of my
eye, you been laughing at me, you been acting like you
admire the candy I been eating, Diamonds and Pearls,
and all those, but what you really been doing is laughing at me, I know you guys from Bitlis, you always make
fun of a fellow, and all the time he thinks you're a pal,

you ain't no pal of mine, Willie, as long as you're going
to laugh behind my back."

"*No,* Eddie. I been jealous."

"You been a *little* jealous, I know, but I never notice
you buying two, three candy bars a night, sometimes
four, you guys from Bitlis don't throw away money on
luxuries, you're famous for being tight, while us jack-
asses from Harpoot, we spend the stuff as fast as it comes
in, and the hell with you from now on, Willie, I'm not
going to show you the wrappers any more."

"Ah, come on, Eddie, I know you had a real good one
on that delivery, let me see the wrapper, I won't tell anybody you been eating up your pay."

Sure enough he reaches into the inside pocket of his
blue coat and comes out with a carefully folded wrapper,
unfolds it, all crazy blue with flashes of red charging
through it, and he keeps looking at me out of the corner
of his eye, but the dazzling thing is just a little too much
for him to care if I *am* laughing, inside of course, where
he can never see it and know for sure. He just stands
there and admires the wrapper: Iceland Fire.

"It's the best yet, Eddie. Thanks a lot."

"I had it from just a little past Stanislaus all the way
to Maroa."

"Boy, I bet it was good."

"Hot and cold, just like it says, hot and cold, one of
the best. Damn you, Willie, you're laughing at me, I
know you are, I can't *see* you, but that's the way you
guys from Bitlis are, you keep it inside."

"*Laughing,* Eddie? I'm crying because I can't afford
to eat that kind of stuff."

But the kind of stuff I *could* afford to eat wasn't so
bad, either. Food, that is. It's the stuff you have *got* to
have, of course. You can't get through one little old day

without it, let alone a week, although one time when I was an old man of forty I only drank for a month, but then I *did* drink, and the fact is I sneaked in a steak now and then, too.

At the orphanage the best was meat pie. Tapioca was poison. We hated it, everybody in the place hated it, I actually didn't like the flavor of it, or rather the flat pointless *lack* of flavor of it, but I ate it every time, I emptied my bowl, and if there had been more I would have had more, too, hating every bit of it.

Well, we were growing, you see, and they knew it, and they knew we'd eat anything they put in front of us, because we had to have something, and we would take whatever we could get. The orphanage people had a tight budget to keep, so of course we couldn't expect anything fancy, it had to be basic, it had to have bulk, it had to cost little, it had to take up space. But don't get the idea some of the stuff wasn't great, because that would be a lie, and as far as possible I don't want to lie about the people at the orphanage.

The Irish cook, for instance. It would be impossible for me to do anything but honor her memory, for she loved us, she loved every one of us, every big hungry mouth and big empty stomach. At every meal she stood in the doorway of the kitchen and just watched us put the stuff away, which *she* had cooked for us. She did baked macaroni real good, too.

Breakfast had to be some kind of hot cereal of course, with milk, and nobody could knock that, and cocoa, as we called it, and fresh bread and butter. The way you did it was to spread butter on the bread and dunk it into the hot cocoa and then slop it quickly into the mouth, for the mixing of the mushy bread, the melting butter, and the hot chocolate flavor, all of which blend

together in a very satisfying way. Sometimes she baked
a million biscuits and that was something we loved, too:
again with all kinds of melting butter in there, and
honey if there was honey set out on the table, and if not,
whatever it was, excepting catsup. She made great corn-
bread, too, for breakfast, lunch, and sometimes for supper, too. She was great on pork and beans, too, and this
was always a favorite. Her hash was better than any hash
I have ever found anywhere, and so was her meat loaf.
You may have noticed that the things were made out of
stuff that is never expensive, but she transformed that
stuff into great steaming pots and pans full of what we
wanted. Nobody ever asked anybody to eat in that place,
because it made you grow, a little for mama, a little for
papa, a little for Jesus, or anything like that. God help
us if the word was out that there would be seconds as
long as it lasted, because that meant the fastest eating
anybody ever saw. The stuff disappeared almost before
everybody was seated, or rather before the starting bell
had stopped ringing, and I mean, specifically, the stuff
on my own plate, whereupon the plate shot out for
more, and more was put there. Now, for some preposterous reason, poultry wasn't on the table very often,
most likely because it was too expensive for the budget,
and so the eating of chicken came to be associated with
the dining of the rich, with what we used to call society
people. We got chicken or turkey, by official vote or
decree, on Thanksgiving Day, Christmas Day, and possibly on Easter, although I'm not sure. I know that if
we got it, it was a special occasion. In my first play, *My
Heart's in the Highlands,* the poet's little son Johnny
is talking to the boy who delivers newspapers in that
part of town every morning. Johnny brags that he has
eaten chicken, and so the paper boy takes pride in the

fact that *he* has, too—*twice*. Old George Jean Nathan got a big kick out of that.

"Why chicken?" he said with his high-pitched voice. "Why not something *fit* to eat?"

He hated chicken.

"What's more," he said one day, "I hate people who *don't* hate chicken."

Now, what else did that great Irish lady prepare that I had better remember with tender reverence and deep and everlasting admiration and gratitude? She's gone, dear woman, let this be for Ireland, for all Irish cooks, for the cooks in all institutions, Irish or otherwise, who do not hate the inmates, who love them, children, criminals, the sick, the mad, or the aged. To all captured and imprisoned, in all of the institutions, greetings, and a sincere prayer for a decent cook.

Rhubarb—she stewed rhubarb real nicely, cooked but not mushy, the color a magnificent red and white, the juice transparent but sweet and tart at once. Well, that was pretty much what it was at the orphanage.

Then came Fresno, the home cooking, the food of Armenia, the famous dishes of Bitlis. Well, of course you know there are several basic foods among the Armenians, as well as among the Turks, Kurds, Arabs, Persians, Greeks, Georgians, Roumanians, Bulgarians, and two or three dozen other tribes, all the way from the Black Sea to the Siberian shores of the Pacific: yogurt and pilaf, or sour milk and rice, for instance. There are small differences in how the stuff is made, but these two items are basic. If you make the yogurt out of goat's milk, you get a different yogurt than the more common yogurt of cow's milk. And so it is with the milk of other animals. Also common to all of these people is lamb roasted on skewers over a no-longer flaming fire, or shish-kebab. *Shish* is Turkish for spear, and *kebab* is Turkish for cut-up lamb. *Tass-kebab* would therefore be cut-up lamb cooked in a tass, or pan. And so on. On a spear it would go like this, more or less, for flavor and variety: a piece of meat, a piece of bell pepper, onion, tomato, and then another piece of meat, and so on, depending on what you had plentiest of. And so that sort of eating was routine for me in Fresno, excepting the shish-kebab, which had to wait for a family picnic, or a whole big Armenian picnic, because you had to prepare it right if you really wanted it to be what it ought to be.

Now, there is something the Armenians and the Turks and Kurds, and surely the Arabs and a few other people, consider basic, too: the Armenians call it bulghour. This is a brown cereal. It's boiled cracked wheat dried brown in the sun. If the wheat is cracked into a fairly large size, it is used for pilaf. I like it far better than I like rice, which I like quite well. You can do anything with bulghour, mix anything with it, that is, but the usual procedure is to fry a couple of cups of it in butter, pour over a couple of cups of clear broth of any kind, or if there is no broth, boiling water, and cut up two or three big brown onions into it, and eat it steaming hot with yogurt. This is the favorite dish of the peasants everywhere, who generally have at least seven or eight kids, and there is said to be a relationship between the eating of this dish and the number of kids in the family.

My mother used to send me to Chinatown, to the famous Japanese fish dealer over there, Takamura, who every Saturday got in a good supply of a small fish that my mother fried and ate with bulghour. For a dime there was enough fish for the whole family, two pounds, a couple of hundred little fish, to be eaten without taking out their insides or removing their heads.

The wheat that was cracked small was mixed with ground meat to make meatballs of all kinds, solid, or with a stuffing made of pomegranate seeds, or to stuff into tomatoes, bell peppers, squash, zuccini, pumpkin, eggplant, and to wrap grape leaves around. In Armenia they stuff apples and quince, too, but that wasn't anything that was done in my house. Dried apricots and peaches went into thick meaty stews to cut the heavy flavor of the meat and garlic and dried eggplant and okra and whatever else might be in there, but apples and quince were not used in that way. They *could* be, of course. The best cooking comes from necessity. You use what you have and you find out how to use it well.

The favorite dish at my house was what the people of Bitlis call Tut-too. Perhaps that isn't the spelling likeliest to help you get the pronunciation of it, but it's said swiftly, with the accent on the last syllable. There is almost no first syllable, actually. The word means sour, or tart. Take a big cabbage, cut it up big or small or both, put it in a crock, throw some salt in there, a piece of bread, or a little dry yeast, pour warm water over the stuff until the water is near the top of the crock, then place a dish over the stuff, and place a weight on the dish to press the solid stuff down. We always used a rock about the size of a big eggplant. After seven, eight, or nine days the stuff is sharp, it has gone sour, but nothing like sauerkraut, something else, in my opinion something much better. The juice deeply satisfies thirst, and is considered an invigorating tonic. Now, if you have other stuff, put other stuff in there with the cut-up cabbage, too: turnip greens especially, celery, green tomatoes, and all like that. It's good raw, the juice is always good cold, but the stuff is prepared pretty much with the intention of cooking this great dish I am speaking of: Tut-too.

In my family there were only five of us, but two of us were very good eaters, that is, my brother and myself, so my mother used a large pot, three gallons or more.

First, she put a gallon of the sour juice in there, and half a gallon of water because that much of the liquid would boil away in the cooking. Into the juice she dumped three or four pounds of cut-up shoulder of lamb, big chunks, bone and all. When the lamb had cooked for half an hour or so, or a little less, she added three or four pounds of the sour cabbage, and a cup of washed *gorgote:* well, *gorgote* might be barley, but I'm not sure. It cooks in there, opens up, and is a very important part of the dish. It *ought* to be in there. Then six or seven big tomatoes are cut up and put in there, and after the whole thing has stewed for an hour or more you have got it. If there is any left over, it is always better the second day. It is eaten steaming hot. In the winter it is great.

Sherwood Anderson in *A Story-Teller's Story* spoke of eating cabbage soup at his house almost every day because hoodlums in his neighborhood used to throw cabbages at his front door, onto his porch, and his mother, instead of being offended by the intended insult, gathered the cabbages and cooked them. I liked that.

Lamb's head was cooked in a lot of water, but my brother wouldn't eat it, because he couldn't stand the head looking at him that way. This also was a favorite of the peasants in Bitlis, called Pah-chah. In addition to the garlic in which the head is cooked, mashed garlic in water is added to the dish at the time of eating, and so you've got a strong dish on two accounts: the strong broth and the strong garlic. The peasants generally ate it on Sunday morning so that by evening it would be digested and they would be sure to sleep well.

Armenian bread was baked all the time at my house, in all of its forms: the rolled out flat bread, thinner than cardboard, the loaves, called Bahgh-arch, and the various breads with a great deal of oil or fat of one kind or another in them, called Gah-tah.

Now, when it was a day for the baking of bread, my mother would be up very early to get to it. She could easily have gotten up three hours later in the wintertime when there was no work at the fruit-packing houses, but she didn't feel bread was being baked unless she got up in the dark, at five, summer or winter, and went to work. By the time the rest of us were up and ready for breakfast her work was finished and the house was full of the smell of freshly baked bread, and the whole pleasant warmth of it, as it had been for several hours, while we slept. When we sat down to eat, though, we got the real treat of Bread Baking Day. This is called Tazhah-hotz, or new-bread, and this is how it is made. Take a handful of the bread dough, flatten it to a thickness of a little under an inch, and drop it into a frying pan in which any kind of fat you use, or butter, is very hot. In a few minutes one side will be a handsome golden brown. Turn it over until the other side is the same, about six minutes all told. Now, break the thing, open up a pretty good-sized piece, and into the opening stuff white Armenian cheese. Drink tea with it. *Only* tea. Cocoa or coffee or anything else would make a mess of

it. Hot, sharp, brisk, weak tea, after the manner of all
of the tea-drinking peoples, excepting the British, who
regard tea as coffee, to which they add milk.

The roasts were all lamb: shoulder, leg, and stuffed
breast, which is a truly great dish, very hot, or cold, generally hot first, and the left-over portion cold, because
certain roasts, if in fact not all of them, are nullified by
a second roasting. The stuffing is a basic rice, with whatever you fancy: dried apricots, raisins, dry or fresh mint,
chopped heart and liver, chopped meat, whatever you've
got that wouldn't be half so good by itself and shouldn't
be wasted. To be on the safe side the rice might be
boiled for ten minutes before making the stuffing, so it
will be a fine cooked part of the roast.

24 The Millionaires

Well, that's a *little* of what we used to eat. Even so,
my brother and I sometimes imagined the food we were
eating wasn't high-class. We never suspected it was the
greatest food in the world, and of course you must understand I have mentioned only the basic stuff. There
was a lot of special-occasion stuff, but the hell with it.
We ate, we ate good, but we wanted to eat differently,
like the Americans did, and so one summer when my
mother was working at Guggenheim's, packing figs,
and there was a lot of overtime work, with extra pay
for it, and she wasn't getting home until late, sometimes
at ten, sometimes even later, she gave us permission to
eat supper together in a restaurant in town. Within reason, you understand. And we understood. It had been
our own idea to keep it within reason, not hers.

We didn't expect to eat in a fancy restaurant where
the six-course meal cost anywhere from twenty-five to
forty cents. They wouldn't let us sit down in a restaurant like that, most likely, so we scouted the various
inexpensive restaurants, and settled for The O.K. on
Kern Street, between Jay and Van Ness. This was
Chinese-owned-and-operated, but American food exclu-
sively, five courses, ten cents, the favorite supper res-

taurant of day-laborers with no money to throw away. All counter, no tables.

Well, who will ever forget the first time we went in there and found two free places and sat on the stools and waited to have our first meal in a restaurant?

My brother was all for examining a menu, like he had seen in the movies, but before he could find one the Chinese waiter came trotting up with two bowls of soup. Dish-water, but my brother said it was great, and after the third spoonful I didn't mind it too much, either. Next came a plate of some kind of stew, cat stew apparently, but we were in a restaurant at any rate, we were being served, and we were hungry, so we ate the cat stew, and the three slices of beets for salad, and then came the dessert: bread-pudding, the bread not quite transformed from bread into pudding. Well, we had had a lot of experience with bread-pudding at the orphanage, and this just *wasn't* bread-pudding. There was a little dab of something red over it, not quite liquid, not quite solid, something out of cornstarch probably, but with sugar in it. We ate that, too, the same as all the day-laborers in there, and finally came a chance to choose: coffee or tea? I think I said milk, and the Chinese said very quickly, "No milk, no milk—coffee or tea?"

So we took tea, got up, paid our dime apiece, put a toothpick apiece in our mouths, and walked out to Kern Street like a couple of characters in a Paramount Picture.

We said it was good, we said it was great, we wondered how the Chinese could afford to dish out a meal like that for a dime. And the next night after we had sold all our papers, around half-past eight or nine, we went in there again and ate the same meal, except that instead of cat stew, it was some other kind of stew, possibly dog stew. Again we said it was great, and we walked home like millionaires, men of the world, diners in restaurants.

After the fourth night, though, I said, "Henry, let's not eat that dime dinner, let's go home and make something ourselves."

Well, he was crazy about the idea, because that food was killing him, too.

And so we gave up that premature venture into lordliness and went home. The place was loaded with the makings of anything we might care to eat.

Henry made bulghour pilaf, and I made a salad, and we sat down and ate the stuff, and my sisters hung around telling us they could have done it much better, and from now on if we weren't going to eat in town they would have stuff waiting for us, but we told them to keep out of it, we wanted to make our own stuff. They were both working, too: the oldest at Gottschalk's as a secretary and the youngest at Woolworth's selling stuff, and they were pretty tired when they got home, and all we wanted them to do was take life easy in the parlor playing the piano and singing while we got our own stuff.

When my mother got home that first night at half past ten she looked at the pan that Henry had cooked the bulghour in. There was a little left in there, so she sat down and put some yogurt on it, and she said, "Who cooked this bulghour?"

Henry said, "I did."

"Where you find out how to cook such good bulghour, Henry?"

"Right here. It's very simple."

And of course it is. All you've got to be is good and hungry.

We paid a dollar ninety-five one time for an ice-cream machine, but it was a flop. Too much trouble, and the stuff *wasn't* ice cream. We went back to lemonade, and good old plain cold watermelon.

For me, though, the greatest meal in the whole world for a summer night was cold grapes, flat bread, white cheese, mint, bell peppers, green onions, tomatoes, cucumbers, and cold water.

25   The Writer

Well, what happens? Might one be permitted to ask? What happens to a man? Does anything at all actually happen to him, or is it always something happening to somebody else, who carries his name? And what about the alias boys? The multitudes who have a true name but choose another, moving from George to Tex, or from Albert to Pat, or from Smith to Bashibazukian? And the boys who are wanted in Georgia, Texas, or Alberta for forgery, and move along from Walter Dill to L. D. Dooley? And a week later to Robert M. Phillips?

Does birth happen to a man, and dispute, travel, and sleep, sorrow, envy, and regret?

The moon is sinking in the sea? Is that all that happens, actually?

What happens to dentists to make them become dentists? Are they sincere? Or do they do it for the money?

Frank Norris wrote a whole novel about a dentist, a looneyboy named McTeague.

Well, long before I *smelled* Fresno, young Frank Norris went down there from San Francisco to gather material for one or another of his novels: not *The Pit,* most likely, and not *The Octopus,* but something about the Southern Pacific, the old S.P., only a stone's throw from the house I mentioned a moment ago on H Street.

I suppose Frank was twenty-six or twenty-seven at the time. He was interested, he was looking for the truth and a fight. He worked hard and he got the books out, but I wonder if he knew how to write. One day back there in the days of the streets of San Francisco, not long after my first visit to New York, I found a book by Frank Norris on a five-cent rack outside a second-hand bookstore on Market Street. I bought the book and read a page or two here and there and put it aside, and then one day ten years later, long after I had had a couple of books of my own published, I picked it up again and read a whole long story in it, about a writer who was a gambler, liked to play poker, but always lost. Lost his girl, lost his friends, lost his identity, lost his zest for less exciting activities, lost his enthusiasm for people, lost his faith in writing, and I thought, "Hey, it looks like this boy was a gambler, too."

For by that time I was all-out in that area, and I knew Frank Norris was writing about himself. Well, the writing really wasn't any good, but it was better than anything his brother ever wrote.

Well, now, why did *Frank* gamble? He came from a good family. He had talent, enough for all practical purposes, at any rate. He had a wide circle of friends, he enjoyed good health, he was handsome, and he had made a pretty good name for himself as a realistic writer, as they used to put it. Zola may have put it in French, *"Le réalisme, c'est tout."* Of course that's my own invention. It doesn't even *look* right, but it may give you the idea, especially if you don't read or speak French, as I don't. What it probably means is: "Realism is all." And that of course means nothing, because if you'll move in close here I'll just whisper something to you, but please promise not to tell little children: *"All* is not all."

There's more, there's always more, and of course being this gambler that I am, and this death-defying daredevil that I am, I'm interested in the more.

Of course, by the time I had paid a nickel for Frank's book, Frank was dead.

I love books, I love buying books for a nickel, I love studying them, I love keeping them, I love thinking about the writers who wrote them, and about the writing itself, which is almost always bad, except here and there where it is suddenly good.

Frank Norris was good quite frequently, but not as frequently as Jack London, and I believe they knew each other.

I liked Jack London a lot, but as the years went by and I tried to figure out his life, and his suicide, I had to decide he must have been driven phoney somewhere along the line. He got involved with this woman he presumed to be toney who dragged him away from a perfectly good wife and a couple of kids, or at any rate a couple of perfectly good kids. Maybe his wife didn't know how not to give him a bad time, and this new woman sent him letters full of Annie Besant talk about her soul and his soul and eternity, and damned if Jack didn't go to work and write the same kind of stuff in reply. And she needed to show him off and have him become a big landowner and the owner of a yacht and the drinking friend of everybody who was anybody. What happens to a man? Was she good in the hay? How good could she *be,* sending letters like that? And had there *never* been any others that good for him?

I didn't get it. I gathered that what he really wanted

very deeply was to be accepted by people he considered nice, and this was a real kick in the teeth to me. I had always imagined he had been with the people all the way. Well, *what* people, for the love of God? Why, all of the people who need, and I don't care *what* they need. If they need, you've got to be with them. The children of the rich can need as much as the children of the poor, maybe more.

Joaquin Miller knew Jack London, too, and I almost knew Joaquin Miller. He lived half a mile up in the hills just back of the orphanage, and my brother saw him and spoke to him. A whole gang of older boys was officially received by him, and he acted like God. He was a real phoney, all bearded that way, and trying to keep growing boys from knowing how really stupid he was, like all the rest of us. He had fooled quite a lot of people, especially the upper crust of London. He took them by storm.

That was the trend in those days. The California writers invaded London wearing cowboy pants and two six-shooters in holsters, and had themselves a great time with Lords and Ladies.

Bret Harte went along and stayed the rest of his life, with an abandoned wife and kids in America.

Best of all, though, was Ambrose Bierce, and it was Joaquin Miller himself who urged Bierce to go to London, and helped him go. Nobody could touch Bierce of that crowd when it came to wit, honesty, intelligence, decent scorn and disbelief, and the ability to write, not even Mark Twain, who also went along, and murdered them.

There was a touch of the phoney in all of them, excepting Bierce, and God knows nobody ever knew him well enough to crack him. Newton Harrison, the night

Wire Chief at Postal Telegraph in Fresno, used to tell me about Bierce in San Francisco when Bierce wrote for *The Examiner*. He was a loner. He went to Mexico to join Pancho Villa and disappeared. Nobody was sent to Mexico by a newspaper, nobody found him living quietly and proudly with the honest savages, nobody walked up to him and said, "Mr. Bierce, I presume." They said he may have been killed. They say a lot of things. They don't know.

They all wrote for a magazine called *The Overland Monthly*, and so I wrote for it, too. When I was seventeen, and still in Fresno, they accepted a story, and I was sure I was on my way, but I wasn't. They couldn't pay, either, and more than anything else in the world I wanted a check for writing, to prove a point. Simple people believe a writer gets a million dollars for every short story that's published in a magazine, but the fact is that if a magazine can pay at all, they can pay only a small sum. If they can't, they say so, and they ask if they should return the story.

It wasn't a bad story, either, but the hell with it.

What happens to a man? Why does he gamble? Why does he want to be liked by rich people? Why does he try to act like God? Why does he leave his wife and kids for a woman who's full of mystical posing? Why does he wear cowboy pants and two guns in London when he has never had anything to do with cattle or cattle rustlers?

It was silly, and very little else, to see the story in *The Overland Monthly*, at least ten years after the death of the last of that gang, and at least half a century after their good days.

The rest of the stuff in the magazine nearly drove me nuts: silly journalistic pieces about somebody who was doing nicely in the cement business, or stuff about a

new store that had just been opened in Daly City, with
the owner standing out front, a family of smartly dressed
window-dummies in the window looking more alive
than the owner, or the story of Yosemite National Park,
with photographs.

Not one piece of writing in the whole issue.

Well, if being printed made you a writer, I was certainly a writer, but I didn't believe it.

I was a writer all right, I knew I was a writer as soon
as I had finally learned to read and write. I knew I
would always write, for the surprise of what I might
write, if for no other reason. And from the time I had
studied my father's home-made notebooks, I knew it
was up to me to write better than he had.

Something was the matter. I didn't realize what it was
at the time, and the fact is I didn't realize for years.

The flaw was that there were no readers.

My father had had none, and now I had none, too.

I read the story, but as I read it I knew nobody else
was reading it. I wanted somebody else to read it, too.
Anybody else, almost, but preferably somebody with a
little brains who might just know straight off that here
was a new California writer, seventeen years old.

Nothing. Not a word from anybody.

The moon is sinking in the sea.

And it isn't that Aram was mistaken, either. He
wasn't. He wasn't interested, and neither was anybody
else. This was the West, and all those boys who had
never had it so good as when they were getting their
first stories published in *The Overland Monthly,* they
were from the East. And it was the people in the East
who were jumping for joy about *The Celebrated
Jumping Frog of Calaveras County,* not the people of
Calaveras County themselves. *They* didn't even know

there was such a story, or if they did know, they weren't interested. Hell, I was *born* in the West, but what good did it do me?

Who *are* readers? Who are the people who make the difference between a nickel's worth of meaning, as in the book about the gambler by Frank Norris, and precisely a nothing's worth of nothing, as in the story by me in *The Overland Monthly?*

The only readers who are readers, the only readers who mean anything to a work of writing, and therefore possibly a little something to the writer of the work himself, are the readers who read the way writers write: consciously, aware of themselves, aware of the work being read, aware of writing itself, and therefore able to *get* the writing, to know it, to understand what it's all about, what's going on. There are many kinds of writers and many kinds of readers, but the writers who are really writers and the readers who are really readers probably have one thing in common: being on the level without being pompous about it. And it's easy to get off the level, and it's easy to get pompous about just about anything. It happens all the time in writing, and it happens all the time in reading. When a book is read by great numbers of people, it doesn't mean the book is good, but it also doesn't mean it is not good, it only means it is being read by great numbers of people. The writer of the book knows if it's good or bad, because he knows what he can do, what he has done, and what's more important, he knows what other writers have done. If any of my stuff happens to get a lot of readers, as two of my books have, I don't tend to believe I've made it, I tend to wonder who the readers are and why they are reading those two books in such great numbers. Well, one of the books, *My Name Is Aram,* deserves to be read, and can do the reader no harm. But the other one, *The Human Comedy*, is different. There are some lapses in it which many readers like even more than they like the stuff that is at least a little better, and this doesn't please me. If the stuff that went off the level is taken for gospel, as it frequently is, it can do more harm than I want any of my writing ever to do. Now, you might say that the harm is harmless harm, but as for me, the hell with that. I didn't *mean* to go off the level, I meant the opposite. I meant to take a lot of everyday stuff and bring out the drama of it, but near the end of the book I went to work and wrote that it appears to be unavoidable sometimes for people to be killed in a war. I went even further, and tried to demonstrate that the murder of somebody in a war can be a thing of great meaning—to somebody or other, sometime or other. Bullshit—but I was in a hurry, the war was upon me, and I wanted to get this thing out of the way before it got me, which it did soon enough, and the hell with that, too. I fought the United States Army for three years, and I won. I'm sorry for every man who fought, and lost.

What happens? What is it that really happens to a man?

26   The Gambler

In the early days of writing, even after I had become published, I frequently used to remark to myself as I worked, as I wrote a new story, "You're not sticking to the subject. You're wandering away. You're losing it."

Well, it may or may not have been true, but I have found that after I have finished a new work of any kind, in any form, long or short, prose, poetry, play, essay, or whatever, a work in which I have frequently felt that I wasn't sticking to the subject, it has invariably turned out that I *had* stuck to the subject, only differently, perhaps even more effectively than if I had insisted on absolute sticking, so to say. How many subjects *are* there, actually? One? Or is it two? Life? And death?

In any case, when I was eleven years old, I was invited with the rest of my family to dinner at the home of a distant relative, his wife, and seven of the eleven or twelve children she bore him before she died.

The supper was a long time being prepared and served, and I had expected to sit down and eat immediately. For an hour the woman was in the kitchen, alone, at work, having insisted that my mother and my sisters were not to help her. She was used to cooking for many, and this would be no different than any other cooking she had done. Another hour went by, and I kept imagining that she was at work on an enormous meal of some extraordinary kind. I was certainly prepared to fall upon it as soon as it was ready. After another half hour the woman finally emerged from the kitchen bearing a rather small platter on which two or three dozen small fish fried in a batter had been carefully arranged. When I saw the platter, as of course the other fourteen or fifteen hungry people there saw it, I was a little let down, but to make known that I had good manners, I said, "Oh, no, thank you very much, that's too much for me."

No sooner said, though, than dawn's early light, much too late.

Nobody spoke.

The platter was placed at the center of the table, a second platter containing rice was placed beside it, and that was supper—for everybody.

This event was a revelation in my life.

My mother, my sisters, and my brother were kind enough not to speak of the matter after we had left the home of our poor relatives, but after we had reached our own home, I could bear their silence no longer, so I brought up the matter myself. There was hell to pay, of course, not in anything said, but in the eyes, and in the smiles. The more I pointed out how it had been perfectly natural for such a mistake to have been made, the more they agreed, their eyes flashing with sympathy, astonishment, and amusement, even though they were all trying their best not to smile.

Only my mother remained earnest and silent, apparently without effort. When everybody had gone off to bed she said very quietly, "You must see about thinking twice before you speak. For you perhaps it might be in order to think *three* times."

Well, it isn't easy. I never made a dinner-table mistake like that again, but I made a lot of other mistakes.

It wasn't easy for me to think *once* before speaking, not because I couldn't think, but because the situation was simple and didn't call for any thinking, but again and again I was proved mistaken.

I dislike indecision. I prefer to make a mistake than to do nothing. If you make a mistake you at least have the mistake, you can study it, and you can even expect to avoid making a similar mistake the next time that kind of situation comes up. I didn't *need* to think once, because I felt I knew, and most of the time I *did* know, I had not been mistaken about that, I had been mistaken about something else. This is bringing me slowly but in an unavoidably round-about way to gambling. That is to say, *my* gambling, the like of which I have only once or twice witnessed in others: with astonishment, disbelief, and complete scorn for the gambler, because even I could see he was a fool.

Once you have messed with gambling, winning or losing, once you have gone into a gambling house, your goose is cooked, you are no longer good for anything else, except more of the same order of derangement, of total dismissal of time and sequence, for that is basically what gambling is. For the true gambler, that is. For the kind of gambler I was, and probably still am. I certainly would be that kind of gambler if I went back to gambling at all, as I probably shall. Money ceases to be money. A thousand means nothing, ten thousand mean nothing, whether it is dollars, francs, lire, beans, or points. The only thing that means anything is the right or the wrong of it, and myself in relation to right and wrong. The theory is that if I am right I can do no wrong, and I have all too frequently demonstrated the validity of the theory. But I have even more frequently had it brought home to me that if I am wrong, I can do no right, either. And by that time there is some arithmetic to do, which I tend to do with the sobriety I knew as a newsboy, counting the coins in my hand, and then counting my papers, and then counting the coins again, and then the papers again, because a nickel was missing. The arithmetic might reveal, over the years of gambling, beginning on Third Street in San Francisco, that a dollar was missing, five dollars were missing, ten, twenty, fifty, a hundred, a thousand dollars, two thousand, three, five, ten, twenty thousand dollars were missing.

Now, of course, if you lose money at gambling, you haven't got the money any more.

As a losing Presidential candidate once said, "Under our great democratic system, the losing candidate does not win." Everybody understood what he meant, though, and rather admired him for not crying. He meant that the losing candidate offers his congratulations to the winning candidate, but somewhere in the midst of the thought, his loss troubled him, confused him, astonished him, proved to be not yet totally acceptable. He was still in the midst of disbelief. How could it be possible that he had lost, especially in that he had come so near to winning? And so, in his befuddlement, and with an unmistakable courage, perhaps even bravery, and certainly with a good deal of charm, his language became garbled. In an instant, though, he corrected the garbling, speaking off the cuff and quickly, awfully tired, as gamblers who have stopped gambling always are, too, and hoping that the pathos of his position, and of what he had said, might not have been noticed, as losing gamblers hope the real extent of their losses will not become known.

I am not mentioning the names of Presidential candidates, or Presidents, winners or losers, because when they write their lies I don't expect them to use my name. I don't know them and they don't know me. They gamble and I gamble. They win and they lose, and I win and I lose.

But in the end I stop, and I do the necessary arithmetic. If it tells me I have won, I try to find out how much. If it tells me I have lost, I try to decide how I am going to get the lost money back.

Well, you never do. You never get anything back. You always get something, but it isn't back. Getting something back is part of the fantasy of the gambler, and for all I know of Presidential candidates who have lost, who run again, who lose again, but in having lost twice get something, surely something very valuable, too. And finally they don't run again. They decide not to, or they are not permitted to, but again they get something. They certainly get older, as I have gotten older getting various things but not getting back anything, not getting back the money, the time, the abandoned sequence, or anything else I may have lost. I have gotten other things, some of them better than the things lost.

Now, as a poor illustration of this, but not as an apology for folly, for foolishness, for aberration, for illness, for anything we want to call it, I may say that every time I have lost enough money to be deeply annoyed by the enormity of it, which has always been picayune, even when it has been fifty thousand dollars, I have gotten something I could not otherwise have gotten. My money losses are picayune, because there *are* billions of dollars.

If a man has a million or two he remains entirely the same as anybody else in the basic involvement with time, sequence, and the human experience. Money itself is picayune. Even so, every time I have lost, and have been annoyed about the difference between right and wrong, with the edge of the wrong moving to me, I have made up my mind to somehow right the wrong, to balance the imbalance, to earn more than the sum lost.

What's more, I have done so, and it has always been by means of writing.

But the point I am trying to make is that I believe all such writing is writing I would *not* have done had I not lost at gambling.

Hence, while I have not always won back the money lost, I *have* gotten a number of things from *having* lost.

I have sat down and written steadily for a month, and of course *that* is something. The writing has been published, and of course *that* is something, too. I have sometimes been paid more for the writing than I lost at gambling, and *that* is also something.

But most important of all, my annoyance has *conditioned* what I have written. Consequently, I have a new book, a new novel, or a new play, with a style I could not have otherwise put into it. The annoyance about the loss of money, of time and sequence, gave the work its style, and now and then that style has been rare enough to please me.

A lame explanation? *More* than lame—crippled. But maybe it's the truth, too. How should I know? In the meantime, the facts, as they're called. Las Vegas, 1942. Five thousand dollars lost. *The Human Comedy* written. Two hundred and fifty thousand dollars earned. Las Vegas again, 1949. Fifty thousand dollars lost. *Tracy's Tiger, Rock Wagram,* and *The Laughing Mat-*

ter written. No dollars and no cents earned, but I *have* the books, they are there, they are going, they will soon be gone perhaps, but until they are, they are being read and readers are getting something out of them.

The style of *Tracy's Tiger* could not have come from anything but loss, anger, and finally love. But that's another department. In the end, anything worth anything comes from love, even when it looks a lot like hate, as in pretty much all of Bierce.

Every year six or seven people write to ask if I will give them permission to make a play, an opera, a ballet, or a movie out of *Tracy's Tiger,* and I reply and tell them no. Some day it probably will be one of those things, though, and possibly each of them, but in the meantime it is what it is. It could never have come to pass out of plain ordinary health, industry, efficiency, and money in the bank.

I suppose I might say that as a writer I have been a little afraid of money in the bank, as other writers are said to be afraid of losing their ability to write, or of madness, or of indifference, or of ridicule, or of death.

Now, I believe I am speaking truthfully, but if I'm not, I myself will watch it carefully: I do not believe I am afraid of losing any ability I may have, or any ability I may *ever* have had, to write. Such as it is, I have always had it, it is myself, it isn't anything by itself, I don't mind at all if it changes, gets worse, or gets better, or stays the same. It's always there, all it needs is for me to be there with it, on a chair at a table with paper and a typewriter in front of me.

And I don't believe that I am afraid of madness, because madness is also myself, I have always had it, I don't think I would give up my paranoia for anything in the world, I understand it too well, and I'm not yet

sure the specialists understand paranoia in general as
well as I understand mine in particular. All children are
paranoid. It might be a good idea for the specialists to
look into that. I once had in mind writing a story about
a father of four growing boys who kept having bad headaches and went to see a psychiatrist, but of course he
went to see my kind of psychiatrist, a man who didn't
keep the father coming back twice a week for ten years.
In the very first talk with the father the psychiatrist discovered the trouble, and promptly telegraphed his government and the United Nations, urging both organiza-
tions on behalf of his client to cut the comedy, as it was
giving his patient severe frontal lobe disturbances.
(Well, you know what I mean, in any case.) Where do
you find honest psychiatrists like that? Nowhere, but
then *they* get headaches, too, and of course they know
why, too, just as I do. I don't get headaches, I go berserk
in gambling houses.

Why is man in his first years paranoid? And why is
this paranoia the very thing that gives children their
beauty, their dignity, their separateness, their charm,
their very truth? Isn't it because they are in a complex
that *imposes* involvement, even though this involvement
is always dangerous, unpredictable, unknowable, and
charged with betrayal, deception, ignorance, injustice,
disharmony, weariness, despair, and cruel madness? And
isn't it also because each child is *himself* the complex,
or the world, as you prefer, the whole human race, and
the whole human experience, and *suspects* it, and re-
sents it, and is afraid of it?

I never wrote the story about the father and the psychiatrist, of course. I hadn't lost at gambling at the time,
so I didn't *need* to write it. It was only one of six or

seven ideas of the day on which it arrived, and it made me smile. I got the smile out of it, at any rate.

And I don't believe I am afraid of indifference, of becoming indifferent, for I have tried to *insist* upon it, any number of times, as a discipline, in order perhaps to arrive at a fresh form of wisdom, or self-deception or whatever it might be, but I have always failed, in nothing flat.

As for being afraid of ridicule, I knew that kind of fear only when I first began to write. I lived in an awfully practical world, and few members of my immediate family, and none in the whole city itself, would be very likely to notice the typewriter I bought when I was thirteen without feeling impelled to sneer and say, "Who do you think you are?" Or, "What makes you think *you* can write?" Or, "Get a load of who's a writer."

I didn't want to be ridiculous, I didn't want to be ridiculed, but I bought the typewriter. I began to try to write, and I kept the fact to myself. For three or four years I was afraid of being ridiculed, but soon enough I got over it. I didn't imagine I *wouldn't* be ridiculed, I decided it didn't matter. I *had* to write. Whoever *had* to ridicule that fact or anything I happened to write was welcome to do so, and still is.

As for death, I do not believe I have ever been very far from it, and while it may be true that nobody hasn't, that everybody is *always* near death, it may also be true that I have been more aware of it than most others are. And I have been afraid of death, especially foolish death, which had no relation to me, which was not out of my own foolishness, for instance, as death is in a war. I have wanted the right to my own death, however it might come, and whenever it might, suddenly or slowly, or whatever. Of *that* death I have had little fear, but I have had some, perhaps a little, all of the time. Most of the time, though, I have either felt unkillable, which is entirely unreasonable, but not as a *feeling,* or decently resigned to my ignorance about when and how. Now and then I have welcomed death, or at any rate the idea of it, which I have recognized as an inaccuracy at the outset, a confusing of death with peace, as if peace were not accessible to me. But I have never felt any need, or had any wish, or any impulse, to end my own life.

I remember vividly a very cold and rainy night in Fresno when after a long day of selling papers my brother and I were home at last, in our own dry bedroom, and it was time to put ourselves aside for a while in sleep, and how astonished I was when my brother, who was generally full of comedy at such times, remembering people we knew in a way to make me roar with laughter, got under the covers of his bed, in his long underwear, and very earnestly said, "Good night, and I hope to Christ I never wake up."

He meant it, too. A part of him meant it. The next day he was all comedy again, but he always remained the fellow who had said those strange words. He had *that,* too, along with all of the other things he had, and I could see it in his eyes and mouth. It was like having a kind of crazy fortune.

I could never have said it and meant it. The minute he *had* said it, I thought of my father, and I believed my father had said it, I believed my father had said it many times. But it was in the afternoon that he finally died, in broad daylight, and nothing like putting the head down and going to sleep at night. He asked my mother for the water he had been forbidden to drink. He drank it, glass after glass, all he could swallow, trying to quench a thirst that was unquenchable, being death's own, he asked my mother not to beat the kids, and he put his head down and died.

Christ, if he could have seen me in a gambling joint, wouldn't he have jumped? Wouldn't he have thought, "My son is a madman. What happened to my son? He's lucky, he's one of the luckiest men in the world, so why is he mad, too? My son is fifteen now, and he's mad. He's twenty now, and he's mad. He's thirty now, and he's mad. He's forty now, older than I was when I died, but still he's mad. My son is fifty now, and madder than ever. Why? Why isn't he a saint, as I wanted to be, instead of a madman? What happened to my son?"

Well, if my father didn't see me, my mother did, any number of times, when I came staggering home, loud and drunk at daybreak. A few months after the publication of my first book she said, "Had you been no more than a common laborer at peace with the world, it would have pleased me more than this foolish success and madness."

But the fact is I couldn't be at peace with the world, or with myself. Never with the world, and only now and then with myself.

27   The Bath

In the house on San Benito Avenue the bath was at one end of the back porch: a tub and a toilet on a plank floor. The planks were old and broken, and in the winter it was always freezing out there. Hot water didn't come out of a tap. There was no hot water *tank*. You heated the hot water on the kitchen stove. The style of bathing was old country, established by Lucy, who for a time was manager of the baths. Until the time of man, so to put it, she insisted on bathing my brother and me whenever she was staying at our house, which was often enough, as she was fonder of my mother than of her other two daughters, or at any rate fonder of the talk with her, the quiet banter, the memories, the songs, the gossip, the belittling of the pompous and stupid. When it was finally the time of man and she suddenly beheld the evidence of it, she said, "And so here is another man, with everything in its proper place. Will you please be good enough to lean forward so I won't see that terrible thing while I scrub your back?"

She scrubbed with a strong laundry soap called Fels-Naptha and a coarse cloth, but as we moved up in the world there was a better laundry soap called White

King, and finally when we began to deteriorate we used Palmolive.

Bath was never more than once a week. That made sense because getting the hot water was a big deal, but it was also believed to be injurious to the health to bathe more often. The body needed a chance to integrate with the spirit, and if you bathed every other day, for instance, the spirit just didn't have a proper place to lodge itself.

In the tub was a small carved wooden stool brought from the baths of the old country, and the bather sat upon this stool. In front of him was a tub made of galvanized tin, and in this tub was the hot water, directly under the cold water tap. Either the old lady sometimes forgot to add cold water to the hot or didn't think it was necessary, because the water was sometimes a little too hot to bear, and there was howling and jumping. The fact is the water may actually have been only warm but seemed almost boiling because the body was so cold. If there was a jump, old Lucy would grab me behind the neck and sit me down, growling at me that there was no reason for her to imagine I would ever be rich. She would dip the old-country pouring pan, or *tass*, into the galvanized tin tub and pour the hot water over me again. Sure enough, this time the water didn't feel so hot, or I was getting used to being scalded. First came the soaping of the head, and I don't mean just the hair, of which there was always a great deal, I mean the face, the eyes, the nose, the mouth, the ears, the neck. Her hands were rough, strong, and busy, and she kept up a continuous growl about the world and the role of the wise and foolish in it. The head got two soapings and rinsings, and then it was the back, and she wasn't satisfied until it was red. Then she attacked the arms and hands, growling steadily: "All bones and muscle, like a stick. Takoohi, why doesn't he have more substance over his bones?" But she didn't really expect a reply from my mother in the kitchen, getting more water. You could see the dirt in the water at the bottom of the bathtub, and there was always a lot of it. If there *wasn't* a lot, the old lady would be annoyed, perhaps believing she was losing her touch as the world's greatest boy bather, but when there *was* a lot, she took great pride in it, growling, "Do you see it, do you see the dirt, enough dirt for a small vineyard of *alicante* vines?" If she heard her son Aram talking about the stuff he dealt in, she picked up the words and threw them around, and she especially liked the sound of *alicante*. It went well with Armenian, or at any rate with her version of it, which was unique and full of all kinds of inaccuracies and inventions. If annoyed enough, she would invent a word, and on several occasions she invented whole phrases. Her hardest work was done when she pushed the freshly wet and soapy cloth into my hands and growled, "Get to your privates." She would turn her back a moment, or at any rate look aside, singing anything that was going for her at the time, an angry hymn from the silly Protestants, as she called them, or an Armenian patriotic song, or her own version of *Keep the Home Fires Burning*. The whole business was in fun, a performance, if you like, for her own amusement, for *your* own if you were equal to it, but most of all for the amusement of the Eye, or the Witness, to whom she was devoted, who was in fact her only rock. "La la la, la la la, now the feet, get them good, you walk a lot." And then a final and total rinse, the old lady saying as she poured the water slowly over the head, "Ohkh." This is not the same as *Ahkh,* which is a lamentation in a dozen different languages. *Ohkh* means good, *how* good, could anything be better? And so on. Then came a large warm towel, a lot of swift drying, both of us working at that, and then quickly across the ice-cold porch into the warm kitchen.

A large glass of cold water with three teaspoons of sugar stirred into it was always waiting for me to drink immediately upon my arrival in the kitchen. No drink ever tasted better. The drink was called *sharbat,* obviously derived somehow from sherbet, or the other way around. I passed along the custom to my kids when they were little. If somebody forgot about this, my son or my daughter said, "Where's my *sharbat?*"

A bath, in spite of the noise and rudeness, or the vaudeville, was a benediction. After the bath came a complete change of clothes: freshly laundered and ironed long underwear, freshly laundered heavy socks, with all holes darned and no toes sticking out anywhere, freshly laundered and ironed blue cotton shirt, freshly laundered and ironed blue overalls, and everything smelling of good strong laundry soap. The hair was dried in the kitchen, and then combed straight back without any oil. No oil was needed, the hair had its own. A pair of scissors were handed to me for the cutting of the toenails, and then the old lady, or my mother if the old lady wasn't visiting our house, took the scissors and cut the fingernails, but invariably cut the nails of one or two fingers on each hand so far down that they were sore sometimes for a whole day.

"Somebody's got to get the hang of cutting the nails properly." Outraged.

"They'll grow back." Indifferent. "Now get dressed and go in the parlor."

Ten or fifteen minutes later came a second *sharbat,* and it was even better than the first.

It was great to be alive. I've said so here and there, in pretty much the same words, and a lot of people have gotten sick of it. They haven't liked it at all, and they have growled, somewhat after the manner of old Lucy, "You'll never be a writer."

Well, I suppose they never bathed that way. They probably bathed in a proper bathroom every evening or every morning, and they probably used expensive bath soap. They probably didn't get a *sharbat* immediately after the bath, and a second one ten or fifteen minutes later. A bath probably *wasn't* a benediction to them. They were *always* clean, or always *super*-clean, perhaps I ought to say. They never saw enough dirt in the tub for a small vineyard of *alicante* vines. They had it made, and it didn't mean anything to them.

The kitchen stove heated the whole house. There was no other heat. The fuel was sawdust. A truck-load dumped into one of the two barns for three dollars. About two and a half loads a winter. Kindling was junk wood, brought home from wherever it might be found. A little fire stayed in the stove night and day all winter, and the smell of the burning sawdust, the smell of wood oils, cedars, pines, oaks, and other kinds of trees, and the smell of the hot stove, here and there frequently red-hot, was good to breathe. Two big ovens, a great space on top, and the name of it in flashing and proud nickel-plate scroll was Excelsior. The cat rejoiced in the magnificent monument, walking around it, or sprawling easily somewhere near it, to watch the Armenians, some of whom in turn watched the cat, which had picked up the style and manner of them, which understood quite a bit of what they were saying, and every bit of what they were doing. They were living there. And so was the cat, a giant grey tom, easy, powerful, independent, and yet warm and friendly. It was a bit of a nut, too, or genius, as you prefer, especially in the spring and early summer. *Wham,* and it was past the latched screen door as if it were unlatched or wide open, but no damage to screen, door, or cat, just the old violent push to the girls. The cat would be gone for a good three or four days, and then it would come back looking like a wreck and sprawl out and start to heal, the writer of Ecclesiastes himself. All vanity. All sorrow and ignorance. For God's sake, where's the meaning of it, and the dish of milk?

Excelsior and the cat. I got a lot, I learned a lot from
them, but then I got and learned a lot from everything.
I was a writer before I got the hang of the alphabet,
even, because I couldn't help noticing anything that
might be around to notice. The thing itself, the way of
it, and the way of the things among which it was real.
The cats that walked beside the railroad tracks, for instance, were not the same as the cats of the houses, of the
families, of the Armenians. The railroad cats weren't
necessarily homeless, they were hunters, and they looked
it. They were leaner, harder, tougher, and they moved in
a tighter, more elastic way, as if always ready to jump,
either upon a bird, gopher, mouse, or mole, or out of
the way of anything that might be a menace. They were
free and had probably *chosen* to be, since I never heard
of a cat offering itself to a family and being turned
away. We certainly hadn't turned ours away. It came
with the house, more or less. It was certainly living
under it, and we certainly knew it, but we never invited
it in. The cat one day *offered* to come in, and we simply
accepted the offer, so to say.

It was an excellent mouser, but if you've ever watched
a cat toy with a mouse and finally eat it, if you've ever

studied the silent terror of the wee creature, and heard its small bones being crushed in the jaws of the cat, you might very well side with the mouse. You might hate the cat. I was certainly dumbfounded that the cat could play a dirty trick like that. I didn't really imagine that the cat and mouse were playing a game, a perfectly innocent game that gave them both a great deal of pleasure, that was entirely natural and a kind of physical and spiritual calisthenics for each of them, but at the same time I believed, the first time I beheld the game, that the mouse *would* get away, that perhaps the cat would *permit* it to, even: The fact is the cat encouraged the mouse to get away, but the mouse seemed stupid or untrusting or something, because even when the cat turned away, as if bored with the whole game, the mouse *didn't* run. And then at last it *did,* and I began to understand why it hadn't before. The cat was on it in a flash and it was caught again, and the cat's paw saw to it that the mouse remained lively, perhaps hopeful, and now and then the cat smelled the mouse, and the mouse trembled violently. It's an unfair contest of course, but only *after* the mouse has been caught, and a wise mouse doesn't get caught.

Excelsior, the cat, the caught mouse, and us. There we were in America, never to see Bitlis again.

When she was truly old and homesick, and her mind was beginning to wander a little, visiting her daughter in San Francisco, every now and then old Lucy used to say softly, "Girl, wear your shawl and let's go walk to the edge of the brook, and then on to my sister Sima's." Edge of the brook can't be the equivalent of what it is in Armenian, but that was where everybody went for water and a walk in Bitlis.

There we were in Fresno, nine thousand miles and as many years from Bitlis.

When it rained the house leaked into thirteen established places, and always in three or four new places, under which night and day we placed new pots and pans in which to catch the drip. Every time my brother came home and noticed the pots and pans half filled with rain water, he always shouted in English, "For God's sake, what the hell is this? No matter which way you turn there's a pot in front of your foot. If it was oil, we'd be rich. We've got to get the landlord to fix the roof. This is no way to live."

One night a leak began to fall directly on his face, as he slept. He got out of bed and went to the kitchen and soon came back with a pot, which he settled under the drip, moving to the far side of the bed, so the pot would sit safely in the proper place. When I woke up in the morning the pot was almost full. I emptied it and put it back, and then I emptied three or four that were almost full in the parlor. Pretty soon everybody was up, walking to the kitchen sink with a pot of rain water to empty, and then hurrying back with the empty pot.

The landlord was a nice guy and knew he hadn't rented us a mansion. One day he came to the house on his bicycle to put up new paper in the parlor. After he had done the work he said to me, "Please tell your mother that from now on the monthly rent will be reduced two dollars, from twelve to ten." Mr. Barr: English, Scotch, Irish, Welsh, or something like that.

We liked his house in spite of its flaws. We liked the yard with the great old English walnut tree in it, and the two barns, and the lilac trees on the alley side, and the whole empty lot beside the house, which became for the whole neighborhood immediately after we reached the house Henry and Willie's Lot. We liked the front porch, the honeysuckle climbing there—that is how it was, I'm not making it up. The fresh green leaves and golden blossoms of the honeysuckle used to be a joy every spring. The little hummingbirds were all over the place, even building nests in the old vine. We liked the big sycamore tree on the alley side, too, and the hosts of birds in it at sundown every evening, chattering, scolding, and bringing the night.

It was a hell of a house, and we were there for a good three or four years. Just half a block down San Benito was the edge of the playground at Emerson School where I learned to read and write. It was a world. It was a time. It was rough, it was tough, it was murder, it was great, it was magnificent, and the people there, speaking that strange language, the people were us. We lived and we died, and it is all gone now, and if you wanted to, you could say it was never anything. I don't want to.

29   The Fame

As far as I was able to understand the matter, I was famous from the beginning, from birth, but then who isn't? If you're born at all, you're born famous, since in all truth there is no such thing as fame, and if there were, if there were any means by which to be certain of fame in relation to *any* individual, this would be known from no more than the *separateness* of the creature, or if you like his unique isolation. Nobody is like anybody else. The closest father and son imaginable are unalike, and so it is with any mother and daughter.

Each is each, make fame of it if you will, make infamy of it if you will, make anything, everything, or nothing of it, the fact remains that each of anything is unique unto itself. To itself, then, its importance is inevitably enormous, and could be called something else, including fame. The loneliest, ugliest, most rejected, despised creature of any order that lives is beloved of itself, of nature, and of the Witness. The more remote the creature is from community acceptance and similarity the more intense is its belovedness. This goes for individual members of families, for whole families, for people of an area of a country, for a whole nation.

But what I'm trying to get to, for whatever it may be worth, is a recitation of my own self-centeredness, fame, personality, pose, or whatever it might be, from as far back as I can remember. I took pride in myself from the beginning of memory, in the wholeness, the good vision, the good hearing, the swiftness of mind and spirit, the laughter, the fact of *being*.

I *expected* good of myself, perhaps the best, and I was annoyed if I failed, if I seemed ordinary, or inferior. I expected high quality to be inevitable and natural for me. All the same, inferior quality was always at least possible, if not also inevitable and natural—sudden anger about dishonesty in a boy I had considered a friend, for instance. The superior thing, the thing of high quality, would have been *not* to become angry, and probably not even to name the *appearance* as dishonesty. Perhaps it was something else, and only needed time. I expected continuous awareness of a choice in all things. *This* order of quality, or *this*. If the awareness faltered, I didn't like it. To be alive was an enormity not to be slighted. The slighting of it had proved disastrous in the kind of world that had come to be taken for real and unavoidable, and in the kind of relations taken for granted among human beings. I believed from the beginning of remembered experience that I was somebody with an incalculable potential for enlargement, somebody who both knew and could find out, upon whom demands could be made with the expectation of having them fulfilled. After the age of fifteen or sixteen my mother now and then found it in order to remark casually, "Do not imagine that others are as you are. There is also guile."

All the same, it is my experience that the guileless are by that very fact not less *capable* of guile but more. And I am not sure that *having* guile is not finally much more guileless than not having it.

I didn't happen to have it, and I didn't happen to want it, certainly not on the plane of relationships with members of the various branches of my family, friends, acquaintances, strangers, or whoever. I might aspire to a little guile (which would be foolish of course) in my relations with the Entirety. I might hope to be clever in the largest relationships, perhaps out of desperation or even despair, but what I know tells me this is futile.

I felt at the same time, and pretty much constantly, that I was nothing in relation to Enormity, the Unknown, and the Unknowable. I was too vulnerable, too lacking in power, a thing of subtle reality, liable to be blown away without a moment's warning, a migrant with no meaning, no guide, no counsel, no refuge, an entity in continuous transition, a growing thing whose stages of growth always went unnoticed, a fluid and flawed thing. Thus, there could be no extreme vanity in my recognition of myself, if in fact there could be any at all. I did frequently rejoice in the recognition, but I may have gotten that from some of the Protestant hymns I had heard, and knew, and had sung, such as *Joy to the World.* The simple fact was that if the song *wasn't* about me, I couldn't see how it could possibly be about anybody else, including the one I knew it was *supposed* to be about, and good luck to him, too.

None of this was important, it didn't really matter to me, it was never a big deal, it was just so, and so what? It came natural to me from the beginning to want to excel, to try to excel, and finally to excel—but of course I always knew the competition was feeble, and the excelling had been only comparative and not worth bothering to notice, really.

Now, had I lived in another environment, a more cultivated one, for instance, this does not necessarily mean that I would have failed to excel because of the higher competition, or even that I would have grown more fully and in a more heightened manner. These may be immeasurables. By which I mean to say that if somebody who appears to be special is given special attention, care, guidance, and anything else that may seem a good idea, it does not necessarily follow that he shall therefore come to more. And it may very well be that he may come to less. As it was, I came to very little, but I might have come to less, and I will take the time to mention how.

First, by dying literally, or by dying figuratively, because of the special attention, and all the rest of it. Second, by becoming unwittingly too dependent upon the special environment to be able to know the kind of living done by *most* of the people, of being even afraid of being a part of that life, and therefore less of the race itself than any man should be, or in fact less than any man *can* be if he is to live past the age of twenty or so. Third, I do not think any man who is special needs especially to have this fussed over by others, since he is quite capable of managing all the fussing he can abide, all that he needs, which he balances with that unspecialness which is inevitable in anything alive at all, and by which he is truly kept alive: fun, laughter, mischief, play, sport, heedlessness, forgetfulness, indifference, gladness, all for *themselves*.

From the beginning I recognized myself. Still, others recognized me, too, and pretty much all the time. Sometimes this pleased me, sometimes it didn't. One also longs for anonymity and unimportance. All the same, I was always especially pleased when an animal came to me, a haltered horse, a street dog, an alley cat, or an animal in a cage at the zoo, getting up suddenly and coming to the front of the cage to face me, and just stand there and look in total peace and harmony. *These* recognitions I believed to be recognitions by the Witness, through its mute creatures, and I was deeply moved by them, and grateful for them.

I traded a broken dollar watch at the orphanage for a young owl that appeared to be dying, and I got the thing to stay alive and grow. I liked anything that had eyes, for they saw me and I saw them. It is in order to know about the self-centeredness of a child, because we *are* the children we were. Self-centeredness, importance, pose, and fame: every man has them, and it's all right to have them, balanced or not. My living pace was swift, consequently a good deal of my behavior after the age of eight seemed to be arrogant and even rude, although I never intended it to be either.

I was never interested in the obvious, or in the details one takes for granted, and everybody seemed to be addicted to the obvious, being astonished by it, and forever harping about the details which I had long ago weighed, measured, and discarded as irrelevant and useless. If you can measure it, don't. If you can weigh it, it isn't worth the bother. It isn't what you're after. It isn't going to get it. My wisdom was visual and as swift as vision. I looked, I saw, I understood, and I felt, "That's that, where do we go from here?"

At school and even at home I sometimes had the feeling that I was being continuously fallen upon by the slow, who wanted to hold me back, to keep me with them.

Now and then a teacher at Emerson School would snap her fingers under my nose and say, "Where are you *now?*" This made the kids laugh, and it sometimes made me smile, but most of the time it annoyed me deeply.

30   The Pose

If the subject had been Andrew Jackson, for instance,
a great general lying under a tree to rest, and a common
soldier had come along, weary and hungry, and had
flopped down beside him, not knowing that the other
was Andrew Jackson, and had talked about the war as
if to himself or to another entirely like himself, and
Andrew Jackson had given the soldier three of his five
acorns, and they had eaten them together, I would have
been there with them under that tree, listening and
looking, for I knew the story, the legend was meant to
reveal something worth revealing about human size.
The great man is great in that he is never unlike others,
never needs to be recognized, and is actually great in
another dimension entirely, and to another order of
vision.

Of course Andrew Jackson didn't tell the man he was
General Andrew Jackson, and of course he gave the man
more than half of his acorns. And I ate the acorns with
them, even though I wasn't sure what an acorn looked
like. The flavor of the acorns was one of the greatest I
had ever known, even though I had never tasted them.

The small pieces of white bread at church on certain
special occasions were always plain ordinary white bread
to me. I didn't care for it at all, but I didn't mind the

thimble full of red grape juice, because at least there
was enough to wet a mouth desperately dry from boredom. I didn't like the whole jumping pretentiousness
of the thing. It was another big deal, and all I wanted
to know was what did they keep cutting him up for,
and bleeding him? Why didn't they leave him alone, as
all of the sensible people of the time had, so that he
might have grown a little more? He needed to grow.
He needed not to be rushed that way. He had been annoyed too deeply too quickly, so he had had to fly off
the handle with remarks that he himself surely meant
only to reveal his annoyance and the unfortunate ignorance of his inquisitors in *that* dimension. They
weren't ignorant in other dimensions, and he knew it:
he just didn't care for the kind of wisdom they had, he
was after more, and they rushed him to paranoia, delu-
sions, fantasies, and suicide. And ever since, the very
kind of people who annoyed him have harped on who
he was, what he was, what he did, what he said, and
why—all invented out of themselves, their own limited
wisdom, weighing and measuring nothing over and
over.

I liked Andrew Jackson because even though he *could*
have pulled his rank, he was too lazy to bother, but most
of all because he was tired and common and sprawled
under the shade of a tree in the first place, with only
five small acorns by which to hope to satisfy his hunger,
and then gave away three. I don't tend to respect generals, but then I don't believe Andrew Jackson *was* a
general, and I don't think he believed he was, either.
Who were they supposed to be fighting, in the first
place? Was it Indians? Surely he didn't feel he could
take pride in *that*.

I liked Andrew Jackson because I believed him to be

the first American I had heard about who was a man. Not a gentleman—that would have been patronizing. Washington was probably a gentleman, but Jackson, and later Lincoln, were men, period.

Out of the legend, Jackson became great to me, precisely because he only did what anybody decent would have done. Another nameless soldier might have done the same thing, although in that event there would be no legend, and the nameless soldier would not suddenly become named and great. Greatness is the state of not needing to be great, not needing to demonstrate it, not caring to. Andrew Jackson is great in the nameless soldier.

My boyhood pose was almost always in the direction of the worthless and useless. I liked to affect being a kind of person I wasn't and wouldn't really ever care to be, as the boredom of it would surely be too much for me. After seeing Jimmy Valentine crack the safe and bring out the frightened little girl who had been locked in there and doomed, I wanted to be Jimmy Valentine, the man with the most sensitive fingertips in the whole state of Indiana, or wherever it was that Jimmy Valentine revealed who he *really* was, a safe-cracker, a man with a penitentiary record. He placed himself in jeopardy in order to do a supreme kindness, in order to save a life, and what a life, the little girl of the world, that's all—a banker's daughter to be sure but through no fault of her own.

I used to pass a brick building and rub my fingertips on the red brick, the way Jimmy Valentine had done, and then I used to wander into a bank, ready to step forward if anybody happened to be locked in the safe. And it didn't have to be anybody as important as the banker's daughter, although I loved her in a way that

she would never know; it could be anybody—or a dog.
I was ready, my fingertips were raw.

"What do you want in here?" the bank dick said.
"We're not giving away blotters this year."

Or if it wasn't Jimmy Valentine, it would be Jimmy
Murphy, Dario Resta, or Jimmy Chevrolet, the racing
car speed demons.

Or it would be the dancer in the second turn of
vaudeville at the Hippodrome Theatre, Reno, of Reno
and Mary: snappy striped suit, straw hat, cane, and
Mary. *"Goodbye, Mary, I'm going to the war, war,
war."*

What war? What *going?* After the turn you're going
to go out into the streets of Fresno and wander around
with Mary on your arm, enjoying art and life.

How I admired him, though, how I envied his good
luck, his handsome sunshiny personality, his easy soft-
shoe dancing, but most of all his Mary, his beautiful
Mary, the dirty rat, stealing my girl.

Or I thought I'd be Rudolph Valentino, and frequently distended my nostrils, although it only made
me look ridiculous. When Valentino did it in the
movies, though, the women quit, they gave up. And I
tried to tango the way I had seen him tango, dipping
low and swiveling large, but it only made Lucy invent a
brand-new phrase, and order me out of the parlor.

All like that. Later, the pose improved, most likely,
but probably not very much, for whatever the pose
was it had to be based upon the pose of somebody
else, and nobody had ever had a pose that one could
imagine was worth the bother, but the hell with that,
too.

31   The Winner

Old D. D. Davis, the Principal at Emerson School,
thought it would be a good idea to invite Mayor
Toomey to visit us, as he was the biggest man in town
insofar as having been elected by the people to a public
office was concerned, and the Principal wanted to make
a good impression on him. It was decided to have a
contest, a letter-of-invitation writing contest. All letters
to the Mayor were to be written by the pupils of the
fourth, fifth, and sixth grades. As a member of the
fourth grade, I was eligible. The contest was announced
a week ahead of the starting time: a one-hour period
in the English class, called at that time Language, which
is just as good, if not better. Everybody who was at all
interested in the contest heeded the counsel of the various teachers and began to do research about the office
of Mayor, the history of Fresno, the role of the public
school in the development of future leaders, the real if
secret purpose of the American way of life, and six or
seven other things. I was too busy noticing the phoni-
ness of Miss Clifford and D. D. Davis to be interested in
the contest, even though I was open-minded about
Mayor Toomey himself, since I had seen him on a horse
during the Raisin Day Parade of the previous year, and

he had seemed to be a rather shy and simple man of forty or forty-five, stocky and possibly a little on the heavy side. The lore of the city was that he was a poor boy who was incorruptible: he neither accepted bribes from the local underworld nor cleaned up the city, as so many candidates for the office of Mayor *promised* to do, and so many elected Mayors tried to do, or pretended to try to do, but never did. Being a poor boy he probably understood that the matter was not superficial and couldn't be corrected by righteous theory.

When the day of the contest came, I wrote my letter to Mayor Toomey in the first ten minutes of the allotted hour, and handed it in. Miss Clifford was annoyed by this apparent belittlement of the contest, and ordered me to sit quietly and not disturb the serious contestants. I sat and considered amusing ways of killing Miss Clifford, but it was dull work and the hour seemed interminable. At last all of the letters were handed in, with a number of the better-behaved boys and girls rushing about at the last minute to get help from Miss Clifford about historical and moral points they had raised in their letters. She was pleased with this attention, for it gave her the feeling of being a teacher of quality instead of what she actually was: a born boob, and bore.

All letters were turned over to D. D. Davis, who acted as Judge. The letters were not anonymous: every pupil's name was at the top of the page.

The following day Mr. Davis came to our class, squatted twice, after his custom, to relocate his stuff, getting them into a more comfortable area of his underwear. This was a mannerism he scarcely seemed to suspect anyone ever noticed. He was a tall, thin man from somewhere in the Middle West, Ohio, Iowa, or

Kansas, and he looked it. There was hayseed all over him, and he was in the wrong kind of work entirely: the farm was the place for him. The fact is that after he left Education, so to put it, he bought himself and his family of eight or nine boys and girls a small vineyard.

He had long since come to know me from my frequent visits to his office, for various alleged offenses against the orderly procedure of teaching at the school, and he had given me either a bad time of waiting or a strapping, or both. Some of the strappings hurt a lot, and some of them hurt only a little. He made me cry two or three times, not from pain, which every man can prepare himself to accept, but from a weariness of the foolish pattern that had somehow become established for me at the miserable school. In essence, I was asked not to be myself, and I couldn't do that. Not for *long*, at any rate.

Miss Clifford and everybody else in the class waited for Mr. Davis to clear his throat, which he always did before speaking. He generally cleared it twice before speaking momentously. This time he cleared it three times.

Now, it may be strange that it was so, but the fact is that the minute he reached our room, I knew he was going to announce that I had won the contest. I was a little pleased, too, because I felt it proved something, although I didn't know what. I had written a very simple and direct letter, in a very good hand, possibly the clearest in the school, without erasures or misspelled words, since in those days I used only words I was sure of, as I do in these, too, because the words you are sure of are always the best for you. You can certainly say all you need to say with them. Shakespeare's enormous vocabulary is a joy to behold in action, but there appear to have been people in his England who were equal to an enjoyment of such a rich language, and I knew there wasn't any such body in Fresno.

Mr. Davis announced the winner, walked down the aisle to my desk, handed me the letter, and asked me to stand and read it aloud, which I did.

He then took the letter and said, "We hope that when Mayor Toomey receives this letter tomorrow morning he will accept our invitation and come and speak to us."

He did.

We had no Assembly Hall at the school, and so it was the custom on such occasions to gather around the broad plank stairway of the second of the twin buildings of the school. After a few minutes Mayor Toomey, accompanied by Mr. Davis and three or four teachers, came half-way down the stairway, and D. D. Davis introduced him as if he were Patrick Henry, Paul Revere, or the Pope, all of which obviously astonished and annoyed the Mayor, who, when it was finally his turn to speak, said in a conversational tone of voice: "I come from a poor family, as most of you at this school do." And then he went on in this manner for perhaps six minutes—quietly, unimportantly, but earnestly. The other speakers D. D. Davis had eloquently introduced on that plank stairway had always affected high oratorical style, and had been unbearable.

32　The Loser

An extra recess in the school playground followed the Mayor's visit, and that afternoon Miss Clifford sent me to the Principal's office again.

"Well, what is it this time?" D. D. Davis said.

Well, of course it was pretty much the same thing. Miss Clifford couldn't abide me, that's all. She wanted me to be a little more like her idea of what a proper pupil in her classes ought to be and I just couldn't be any such pupil.

"Rudeness, I guess, the same as ever."

"Well, now, what am I going to do with you?"

"Strapping, I guess."

"But it doesn't do any good."

Well, he wasn't mistaken in that.

The first time D. D. Davis had punished me I had been outraged and had spent a week plotting to kill him, but the second time I only hated him for being stupid, for not looking into the matter a little more fully. The third time I felt nothing worse than, "All right, let's get this stupid rigmarole over with."

On that occasion he must have sensed my attitude, because during the strapping, with a leather belt which he kept in a desk drawer, he finally made me cry. I used

to count the strokes: one, that's gone. Two, also gone.
Three, not too bad. Four, it's beginning to hurt a little.
Five, it hurts. Six, it really hurts now, but the hell with
him, I'll take it. Seven, it hurts too much now, but he'll
stop at ten. There's eight already gone. There's nine.
It's all over, ten.

And back to class after a long drink at the fountain
in the hall. I always needed a lot of water. I liked water
in the first place, but whenever I was in trouble I
needed a lot of it.

The time I cried, though, he didn't stop at ten. He
went on to eleven, on to fifteeen, and after that I lost
count, because I was bawling and cursing, which only
made him hit harder, and made me feel I must be an
idiot not to turn, take the strap away, and use it
on him.

This was finally done, in any case, by one of the
three sons of an immigrant from Moush, a boy of enormous strength named Mahshik who later became a
professional wrestler: he picked up D. D. Davis,
slammed him straight through the wood and glass of a
shut window, and dumped him into the playground.
Mahshik was sent to Reform School, of course, but the
ice had been broken, and D. D. Davis thought twice
when his guest was an Armenian boy who was obviously no more addicted to reasonableness than he was.

"Well, now," he said, "if the strappings aren't doing
any good, let's try talking about it—at least this one
time, because of the letter you wrote that brought
Mayor Toomey to our school. Why can't you get along
with Miss Clifford?"

We chatted five or six minutes, and then he brought
the strap out of the drawer of his desk, and for a moment I believed he was the biggest crook in the world,

but he said quickly, "I'll just hit the chair, and you holler a couple of times, will you, so Miss Clifford will be satisfied?"

What I couldn't understand was why he was so determined to satisfy Miss Clifford. The school lore was that every semester he jumped one or another of the teachers, on the leather sofa in his office, but surely he hadn't gotten involved with such a cull, such a reject, as Miss Clifford, and if he had, why?

This mock punishment was ridiculous and I refused to holler.

"Well, just once, just once," he said, and so finally I gave out with a prolonged but obviously bogus howl, not so much to achieve the deception, but out of a kind of unaccountable sympathy for his silly position.

"Thanks," he said, "and now when you go back to class, please try to act punished, will you?"

I wrote about it in one of the stories in the collection called *My Name Is Aram*. D. D. Davis was an entangled man, probably not really vicious, just a little on the ignorant side, and now and then a little bullied by the teachers he had jumped.

I learned to read and write at Emerson School. I learned to read and write in the Public School System of Fresno, of California, but I'll be damned if I'll think well of the school, the system, the city, or the state on *that* account, even now.

The Armenians were considered inferior, they were pushed around, they were hated, and I was an Armenian. I refused to forget it then, and I refuse to forget it now, but not because being an Armenian had, or has, any particular significance.

I flaunted being one of the despised and hated. I wanted the despisers and the haters to be sure they marked clearly who I was, which they did of course.

D. D. Davis, when he was seventy or so, ran into an old classmate of mine at Emerson School who had achieved great success in business and was a millionaire several times over, another Armenian, but always a well-behaved one, never in trouble with anybody on any account.

"Did anybody think Willie would become a writer?" D. D. Davis said. "Did anybody *know* he wasn't just another incorrigible? I did. I didn't think he would be a writer, but I was sure he would be something."

On the last day of school the year I finished at Emerson, I was invited by D. D. Davis to make the speech of welcome to the first Parent-Teachers Association meeting at Emerson School. My family was represented by my sister Zabe. The whole sixth grade classroom, my last classrooom, was full of relatives of kids at the school. They sat, two to a desk, they stood in the aisles, and they stood at the back of the room. They were mainly Armenian women, although there were a number of Syrians and Assyrians, one or two Mexican, Portuguese, and Basque, and the rest were what we used to call Americans.

I had made a few notes for the talk, but I soon forgot the notes, and went along to stuff that was more appropriate for this particular group.

"This place is a different place to every pupil. Every teacher is a different person to every pupil. Something is learned by everybody, although it may not be anything that is being taught by the school and the teacher. All the better. Don't be angry if your kids get into trouble. They may be learning better things than you might think."

Now, I knew that most of the women—there wasn't

one father or brother in the room—couldn't understand English too well, and so on their behalf I spoke very clearly and as slowly as possible.

"If it seems to you that you or your kids are considered strange, different, unattractive, or even inferior, don't believe it, because it's a lie and if you do believe it, you will forget the truth and how to cook and how to keep a happy house."

My sister had tears in her eyes, most likely from amazement and confusion, especially in that I had mixed an earnest tone of voice with a sudden and unexpected remark about cooking. This had been deliberate, because a number of teachers had complained that the Armenians put so much garlic in their cooking that when the boys and girls came back to school after lunch at home the air in every classroom became unfit to breathe. I wrote about that, too. I told a teacher not to ask a whole people to change their cooking, but to open a window. It was too cold to open a window, she claimed, and I suggested it was too cold only if your lunch had been a tuna fish sandwich. Disaster again, of course.

During the recess period after the Parent-Teachers Association talk, D. D. Davis came to the playground just as I came to bat. Three pitches and I was out. Instead of hitting a home-run, I had been deceived by the pitcher three straight times. As I threw down the bat with disgust and walked away, D. D. Davis said, "There goes William Jennings Saroyan. He may not be able to hit, but he sure can talk."

I hated school. I hated that kind of law and order. I hated government. I hated the imprisonment and belittlement of the free and swift individual.

Three times in my life I have been captured: by the

orphanage, by school, and by the Army. I was four years in the orphanage, seven or eight in school, and three in the Army. Each seemed forever, though. But I'm mistaken. The fact is I was captured only once, when I was born, only that capture is also a setting free, which is what this is actually all about. The free prisoner.

33 The Automobile

We know I was great from the beginning, and it gave us a dull pain at the back of the head, so let's meet some other people and animals.

And let them be great, too, or at any rate *possibly* great. At the same time there is no need to ignore the less great, the non-great, the anti-great, the anonymous, the unimportant, the insignificant, the useless, the unfortunate, the ill, the mad, or the wicked.

First, the bum who went walking down the street when I was born. He was O.K.

Second, we've had the immediate members of the family, so we can forget them, too, most likely. The family—who needs it? Always reminding a man who he is, which isn't necessary at all, because he's more, he's a damned sight more, and the hell with the evidence to the contrary.

Third, my father's horse. Now, even though a horse is not a human being, not one of the people, a horse is so much a *part* of people, perhaps it comes to the same thing.

But please don't expect a dashing horse that my father used to leap upon and charge away. Nothing like that at all. I am speaking of the horse that was hitched to the wagon that took us all away from a little house on a little vineyard in Fresno and started us on our way north, first to San Francisco, then south a little to San Jose, and my father's death.

And don't expect me to have known the horse in any wonderful way, either, or even to have looked into its face, the resigned sorrowful face of all old horses, for that wasn't how it was, either.

In fact it was nothing, but the horse *was* a horse.

A messenger in a blue coat went by on a bicycle (and we know I was to wear that same blue coat later on and ride that same wheel and be that same messenger). The movement of the messenger's bike stirred up the soft hot dust, and I breathed the dust. It was good to breathe mixed that way with the scent of heat, of irrigation water in the little grass-choked ditch, of ripening grapes, of the little blossoms on weeds, of time, of my family, of the horse, and of my father coming out of the little house for the last time.

What goes on, boys?

Something goes on. That messenger in the blue coat didn't ride by and stir up the dust for nothing. That dandelion didn't sail lazily through space for nothing. The bird that plummeted into that old olive tree and nearly choked to death on an urgent declaration of some sort didn't do that for nothing.

What goes on?

I didn't know, and nobody was talking.

In the back of the wagon, beside me, seated upon another apple box full of books, my brother wasn't talking, and just ahead of us, where they could hold the frame of the wagon seat, my sisters weren't talking, and my father wasn't, and my mother wasn't, and certainly the horse wasn't.

And then came the answer, spoken by my father: two

clucking sounds that weren't even words. They were spoken not to me but to the horse, which began to act upon them immediately, but with a great deal of effort.

And then finally came the answer in a word, in a word of a language at last, English presumably, again made by my father, but again directed to the horse: Gidyap.

But it was the answer to me, too.

Go.

And the tired old horse went. The troubled young man who had spoken to the horse, he went, too. The tired earth stayed and began to be left behind. The Witness witnessed, the listener listened, the thinker thought, the dust rose from the hooves of the horse, the dust rose from the wheels of the wagon, and there was no getting away from us.

Nobody knew what to say, nobody said anything, but a lot of things moved back and forth among the six people, three male and three female, and back and forth along the dusty road, endless both ways, going or coming, and among the trees by the side of the road, and the vines beyond the road.

Nobody said a word but a lot of things were saying themselves back and forth and once around again. And who was it leaned against his brother and went to sleep, and never remembered the end of that journey, that ride, but never forgot the start of it? It was you know who, of course, two or three months from the age of three, the last member of a whole family, drawing nearer and nearer to dispersion.

His full name was John Wesley Hagen, and with his wife, Lillian Pender, he ran the orphanage. He was a Scot and maybe she was, too. I could abide him but not

her. In front of everybody in the dining room one evening it was necessary for me to get up from my place
and walk twenty yards or so to where he stood waiting,
and because it was *me* he had called, and because I
had gotten up so quickly, and because of the way I
walked, both swift and as if I were loitering, everybody
in the dining room broke into loud laughter. When I
reached him, my cheek felt the impact of his rough
hand, a gesture of affection, for he was smiling, but I
hated him for it.

Lillian Pender painted portraits. I was ordered to sit
for her, so I sat, but she was annoyed, either with me
or with herself, because she could do nothing with it.
She had me back six or seven times but never finished
it. She was from a good family, as the saying is: a better
family than his, for instance, and he was never permitted to forget it. He nearly forgot it now and then,
though, but she always brought him back.

John Forderer was one of the Trustees, or at any rate
something of that kind, a man of thirty-five or so with
a red beard, the favorite of all of the kids because he
really liked them, and he didn't make them feel he
was being a hero about it, either. He came from money,
but he didn't make a nuisance of himself on that account. He was one of the first to buy an automobile,
and he regularly took a load of kids for an exciting
drive.

The talk about Mr. Forderer and the automobile was
all over the place, especially by those who had been
taken on a ride. My turn was coming, everybody would
be taken just as soon as possible, six or seven boys or
girls once a week.

He didn't make it, though, and neither did I. He had
an accident in which he was killed, and a boy of four

or five, whose portrait had only just been finished by Lillian Pender. Did a train hit the thing, or did another automobile, or did it tip over, or did it hit a wall or a tree or a statue, or what? I have forgotten, or I never found out, but I never again saw the man with the red beard. And I never again saw the small boy, who was somebody I either didn't know or couldn't remember, after my time. I can't remember him now, either. Perhaps because that's how it is when somebody little dies. His portrait was printed in color on a postcard, and the older kids were permitted to take the cards around from door to door and sell them, for a fund for his mother, or for a tombstone, or for something.

34   The Foray

One day with Sammy Isaacs and Teddy Dolan I plotted and performed the following adventure, or crime, as it came to be considered: I went into Lillian Pender's studio-office with the intention of asking politely if the three of us, now quite well along in years, six, most likely, might be permitted to have a dozen or more cards each, to take from door to door, too. But nobody was in the studio, and there on her desk was a stack of about a million cards, so I took thirty or forty and went back to where my thoughtful and hopeful friends were waiting. I divvied up the cards in the usual manner, one for you, one for you, and one for me, until there were no more to hand out. And then we took off, staying fairly close together.

Well, the people who answered my own ringing or knocking, I can't include in this gallery of remembered people, because they were only the people who open doors, but I do remember my embarrassment when they cried out, "Oh, you're one of the orphans," and gave me a nickel, or a dime, or a nickel *and* a dime, or a quarter, and took one of the cards. In no time at all I had a pocket full of money, a rather heavy pocket full, and it was the same with Sammy Isaacs and Teddy

Dolan. And so of course we were tempted, we were sorely tempted to spend some, but it rather bothered us to spend the dead little boy's money and so we didn't go berserk, we just bought a nickel's worth of candy each and ate it, and sold more of the cards, and rejoiced in our cleverness, in our daring, our boldness, our fearlessness, our effectiveness and success.

But soon night began to fall and each of us was rich, and perhaps we ought to run away, chuck it all, but in the end we decided perhaps not, perhaps we ought to find our way back, but there directly in front of us was Woolworth's Five and Ten, so we went in and looked at all of the wonderful stuff. Each of us blew another nickel on a pocket knife, but we must have been a long time in there, because when we went out it was night.

We asked various people which way to the orphanage, which way to Peralta Street. Some *almost* knew, some didn't, some took it upon themselves to ask others, and a few wanted to ask the police.

That made us bolt and run, and try to find our way back without any help.

Somebody with an empty wagon told us it would be all right to hop on, so we did, even though we didn't know if he was going in the right *direction* even, and he didn't know, either, but we were *riding*, at any rate.

The streets and houses continued to look wrong, so we finally jumped off and asked a boy of eleven or twelve, and he knew, he said it was far, but he told us how to get there, at any rate. We took off, walking as fast as we could go, because we knew we were in for it. And we *were*. We knew how badly we were in for it the minute we turned up the sloping paved road that curved to the steps of the administration building.

They were waiting for us.

Lillian Pender grabbed my arm and took me into her study. I put all of the money in my pocket on her desk, and the others did the same. She gave us a mean preachment, while John Wesley hovered around, came in and went out, to let her know he'd rather she stopped and didn't suddenly take it into her head to demand that he punish us. She did, though. No supper.

None of us bawled, though. We simply compared our several feelings of outrage, washed, as we had been instructed to do, and sat down in the empty dormitory, while everybody else ate supper. After supper the dormitory became filled, and everybody wanted to know the details of what had happened, so of course we told them. A few of the older boys became righteous and said, "But they've *got* to give these boys supper."

We asked them not to make any more trouble, because while supper would be great all right, we just didn't want any more of what we had had from Lillian Pender.

The Irish cook heard about it, though, and spoke to John Wesley, and finally a messenger came and asked us to follow him but not to make a big deal out of it or anything. He took us to John Wesley who was standing at the kitchen door, chatting with the Irish cook, and when we arrived he permitted her to shove us into the kitchen, to her own little table, and to sit us there. She brought us a bigger and better supper than anybody else had had.

35   The Summerhouse

There was a family one summer that wanted a likely boy, and I was elected. This was a summer custom, and a great many boys and girls went off to these proper homes for a month or two, or for the whole summer.

"Rich people, most likely," I mused. "Might be interesting. Chicken probably three times a day. Intelligent conversation. New ideas, new adventures. Give it a go."

The house was a great dirty shack, that had the worst smell of mould, dust, piss, and decay I had ever breathed. As for the people, they certainly *meant* to be nice enough, but they smelled, too.

Now, of course everybody smells, everybody has his own personal smell, which doesn't necessarily mean that it's bad, although the eighteen-year-old daughter of the family, who was to teach me the ropes, had a smell that I felt even then must surely be all too private.

I couldn't breathe in the place: the air was foul with something worse than dirt. It had something in it of a waste of life that scared me.

Still, I wanted to be grateful, and I made up my mind to be happy and cheerful, but the table was messy, the food was bad, the father was a bore, the mother was sickly, the son of twenty-two had pimples, and I have described the daughter.

Suddenly, after having been in the house only six or seven hours, I began to feel annoyed with whoever it was who had played this dirty trick on me.

If the orphanage was hell, I had at least gotten used to it, I was adjusted to the rigmarole of schedules, I knew what was what, and I could put up with everything in a way that made my real life not entirely bleak and desperate, but this place was a rotten, putrid hell. There was always a slight smell of some kind of strong cleaning fluid at the orphanage, lye or strong soap, but it wasn't *everywhere,* it was just in the lavatory, and while the whole place, all of the buildings, had the smell of an institution, it was nowhere near as bad as this.

All the same, I argued that the people were surely charming and intelligent, the house delightful and a place I would surely soon enjoy being in, the fault must be myself, and if so, I had better see to it, I had better take it slow and easy, and start making profound discoveries about them, and about their home. Tomorrow would be another story, and I would be equal to fulfilling the expectations of the people at the orphanage who had sponsored the event. I would be away for at least a month, perhaps two, and when I returned I would be able to take pride in that fact and to discuss my people with somebody who had also visited somebody.

My place to sleep, though, was in a kind of hall. The bed was broken, the mattress was lumpy, the covers had a rancid mouldy odor, and instead of sleeping all night I fought a long and bitter duel with the world, the orphanage, and myself.

I felt on the one hand that I simply had to find out how to stay, and on the other that I had to get up and put on my clothes and *wait* for morning, and then go straight to the father and tell him I would be much obliged if he would understand that I wanted to go back to the orphanage.

Before breakfast I told him so. I couldn't sit at that table again and try to fool with that food and conversation again.

I was back at the orphanage an hour later.

Why do they do it? Why do silly people take it upon themselves to try to be kind when they have nothing to be kind with, for the love of God?

Part of the orphanage was disappointed in me, in my quick return, part of it was annoyed with me, but the part that mattered was glad I hadn't put up with it: my brother, and my sisters, the oldest of whom was fifteen and said, "They've got their nerve sending you to a place like that. They've got their nerve, I'll say, and they won't get off so easy. I know who did it. Never mind. I'll tell her a thing or two. Do you send my brother to trash?" And so on and so forth.

And of course I knew she meant Lillian Pender. I knew she was sure Lillian Pender had sent *me* to this particular house and family because she hadn't been able to finish her portrait, because John Wesley was always looking for me to go with him to Fruitvale on his horse-and-wagon errands.

I was glad to be back. Another day at that place would have damaged my health forever.

One day there was a crying boy on the porch of a house not far from the orphanage. I saw him up there on my way home from Sequoia School. He was three or four, and I knew something of the worst kind was making him cry. I stood across the street, and looked and listened. Soon the front door opened and four men brought out a casket, to put in the wagon at the curb, thereby driving the boy berserk with disbelief. He didn't want them to go away with whoever was in the casket, most likely his mother or his father, but they went away just the same. They left him on the porch, with a woman who tried unsuccessfully to stop him. Well, I could have told her.

"You can stop his crying only by bringing back to life whoever died, but you can't do that, can you? Nobody can do it, but by God maybe I can do it. Anybody can do something that's possible to do. Well, when you have somebody who's crying like this boy, let's get along and do something impossible, and stop his crying. Let's find out how to do *that.*"

There are a few things that stay, to which a man returns again and again, and the crying boy on the porch is one of these things for me. I have never stopped thinking about his grief. Now, a little girl wouldn't have cried that way. She would not have been that unreasonable. Girls get such things straight quicker than boys. Women resign themselves to the final better than men do. Every little girl is simultaneously mad (in a way that is entirely delightful), and entirely sensible, swift in understanding, and practical: so somebody's dead, so on to the business of living, then. What good are tears?

I was on the boy's side, though, knowing he was mistaken, entirely at fault, and his behavior out of order.

If grief could speak, the burden of his message was thundering and simple: "I know my mother is dead, I know my father is dead, I know the dead always *stay* dead, but I refuse to believe this, I refuse to accept it, you have no right to ask me to believe it just because everybody else has always believed it. I demand the return of my mother, my father. When you meet this demand you need hear me no longer."

37 The Kite

Up in the hills above the orphange lived the West family in a long shack with pretty much the same shape as
their chicken and rabbit runs, and these were my favorite people in the whole world. The pleasant and
casual father and mother and the five boys and one girl,
from eighteen to nine, all of them freckled, the daughter, the first-born, an easy-going beauty who could do
anything her brothers could do but never gave them a
bad time about it.

What they had, almost as a unit, was ease and laughter, a natural and inevitable sense of adventure and
fun. They were interested in everything, but the oldest
boy had a motorcycle that he was forever fixing and
racing around on, with a younger brother or myself
latched on behind him.

They knew all about the hills, the trees, the birds
and animals in the hills, the brooks and streams, the
fish, where to go to catch a snake, where to go to fetch
home a jar of brown slippery water-dogs, as they were
called—salamanders, I suppose.

And they were forever making things, and making
them work: things out of wood and paper, like kites,
which they would have sailing away up in the sky, the
kite fighting the line, and you would see them running

with the fight and stumbling and falling and laughing and roaring out to one another, and hell, they were a family, and every one of them smelled human, and their house smelled civilized, and even the smells that came from the chicken and rabbit runs were good to breathe.

The youngest of the boys and I became pretty good friends, but just lately I've become a little unsure of his name, which goes to show you what time will do. Roy? Melvin? Hell, I've forgotten it. He used to come loping along to the orphanage grounds and gardens looking for me or for other of his friends, and if we were working in the vegetable garden, turning up and gathering potatoes, he'd get in with us and work and talk and laugh as if he were one of the orphanage kids like the rest of us, and there weren't many boys in that part of Oakland who did that. Just the West Boys, as they were called.

One or another of them would go to somebody official and ask if somebody or other could go up to their house until suppertime, and that's how I was allowed to go a dozen times or more. But we *saw* them all the time, they were around, they were members of a full family, and they were good to see. It was good to know there *were* full families like that.

38   The Debt

I began a moment ago by implying there was something
to say, something to be said, something to *have* said
after half a century since the arrival of memory in my
life, since the arrival therefore of myself into it. I have
tried to say, I have meant to say, I have believed I
might say, but I know I haven't said, and while it
doesn't trouble me, or at any rate not violently, as it
would have troubled me thirty-five years ago when I
wanted to say everything in one swift inevitable book,
it also doesn't please me, and I feel that I must try
again.

We are here. We have been here for some time. Before reaching here we were not here for a long time, and
after we leave here we shall be away from here for a
long time.

What did we do?

Eat?

Yes, we ate.

Talk?

Yes, we talked.

Work?

Yes, we worked.

Anything else?

Yes, we did other things, too.

When I think of the writing of the good writers, I am appalled. They know how to write, they know how to make the saying of nothing seem like the saying of something, and now and then like the saying of everything, but my writing is like my drawing, like my piano-playing, like my walking, all in a straight line, and pretty much from nothing and nowhere to nothing and nowhere, and back again.

Well, don't just stand there, *say anything*.

Hello, folks.

Is that it?

Well, it's a start, perhaps.

Goodbye, folks.

Well, *that's* also a start, of sorts.

Now, if you had only been a general in the war, you could tell the folks about *that*.

Folks, I *wasn't* a general in the war, and I'll tell you about it.

Folks, it was a great responsibility not having twenty million men under my supervision, because if you want to know the truth I don't have any particular ability as a non-supervisor. Folks, I'm really a song-writer.

Gad, the weight of the books, the weight of the memoirs of generals.

I have so far mainly considered the earliest times, not especially intending to do so, but falling into it, as it were, perhaps because when the nature of your work is to remember, you tend to start at or near the beginning, and then to go back again and again, expecting most likely to find out a little more fully why you have become estranged, why you are one place and the world another, as the Armenian saying is. It means one of you is mistaken, the world or yourself. And so perhaps now it might be in order to begin at the other end, and to say the nothing that must be said about the actual now, the actual present, for me.

I live in Paris, where I have lived on and off for a year and a half. The on and off of it is that last year at this time I sailed from Genoa to Sydney, and from there flew to San Francisco, and from there took a train to New York, and from there sailed back to Paris.

From the last day of October last year to the first day of December I sailed from the old Mediterranean city to the capital of the littlest continent, the island continent, the continent of the marsupials, down under, as they say, the continent I call *Joey in the Pouch*. I was running away from the quicksand of gambling, the quicksand and lightning of myself, the quicksand, lightning, and snowstorm of my family, my people, my lineage, the unknown, the unknowable Saroyans.

The entire month of November I was at sea, with short stops here and there. On this very day last year, for instance, November 15th, I walked in Djakarta, Indonesia, but that was 1959 and this is 1960, and now I am in Paris, in this fifth-floor flat on Rue Taitbout, back of the Opera, a little past Trinity, a little before Notre Dame de Loret, one of my favorite buildings in Paris, with larger-than-life statues standing around at the top.

This is an ice-cold flat, and while there is a butane heater on rollers to light and to move around in here from place to place, and a small electric heater to plug in, I prefer the cold, but such matters are really none of my business at this time.

The first day in Sydney I found the only game in town, won the equivalent of two thousand dollars in fifteen minutes, and then lost it all back in three hours, along with five or six hundred more.

And then, precisely three months ago, I took a ship from Le Havre to Leningrad, and from there I traveled all over Russia in Europe.

Again I was running away from the quicksand of gambling, but this time, unlike last time, I had run through almost all of the money I had in the world.

In Moscow I went out to the Hippodrome and bet the trotting races, trying to get the hang of what was going on from a program printed in Russian, and of course I wasn't able to get the hang of it. I made losing bets on four races and let it go at that.

Now, I came to Europe to earn the money I need by which to pay the Tax Collector in full, and get him off my back where he's been for fifteen years. It's not his fault he's there, it's my fault, but I don't like him there just the same. I would much rather he got on somebody else's back for a change, and I mean on the back of anybody who knows how to accumulate money, how to keep it, and how to get more.

I haven't been able to keep it so far, but now as the years go by and time grows short I must confess with something very nearly like profound embarrassment that I have finally decided I *must* earn money, I must pay the Tax Collector, and I must find out how to keep money.

Before I went to Australia I was in possession of forty thousand dollars which I had earned soon after reaching Paris, which I had put aside for the Tax Collector. I earned the money by doing what is known as hack writing, but I don't do hack writing, so I will have to call it something else, something more accurate. I wrote a play for a producer of movies. The play is a good play, although I was *hired* to write it. I took what we call an original idea for a story to the producer, and he liked it and asked me to write what is known as a treatment of it. I told him I didn't write treatments, I didn't know what they were. He told me to write a scenario, but I didn't know what a scenario was, either. I told him I knew what a play was and I would go to work for him and write a play, based on the original idea, and he could have somebody else put the play into any form he liked.

My wages were sixty thousand dollars.

The worth of the play is not possible to guess, although it is probably far more than that. It is also probably worth not much more than sixty cents.

The play was a hit in Vienna, and later in Berlin. In the German language, of course. I wrote a cabbage, that is. A cabbage is any writing that is done for money, and doesn't belong to the writer.

As a rule I try not to write cabbages, but I had had no choice.

Now, while sixty thousand dollars isn't a small sum, you must understand that to a maker of movies it is a *very* small sum, for he will pay thirty or forty times as much to others before his film is finished and his flacks make an heroic effort to ram it down the throats of the poor public.

In short, I should have been paid more, but as I was in Europe to make money, I had to put aside any notion of *not* being hired, of not earning something, of not being a hack. I worked like a desperate dog, and wrote a good play.

The writing was *my* writing, and the best I knew how to do. I don't know how to write two ways, one for money, and one for truth. I have got to believe I go for truth every time, even when I am hired and am writing for wages.

And I may say it is contrary to policy for me to *sell* a play. I am only willing to lease it, but this was different. If I didn't start making money and stashing it for the Tax Collector I might *never* get him off my back.

Later in 1959, for the same producer, I took some writing he owned, which was useless to him as it stood, and I transformed it into another play, and this time my wages were twenty thousand dollars. Of its kind—a kind I don't like—this was a good play, too, but my connection with it was secondary, or less than that. The original idea of it was based upon a courtroom novel, which in turn had been adapted into a play, which in turn I had made over into a new play, hack work of the most unappealing order for me, but again I had had no choice.

As a matter of fact, my son and my daughter were with me in Paris at that time, in a big rented apartment, and I took the matter up with them. After three or four days of thinking about it, from every angle, my daughter, then thirteen, said, "It's a job, like any other job. Sometimes a writer has got to take a job, too, Papa. Do it."

And my son, then fifteen, said, "It's a lot of money from one point of view, and from another it's nothing. A lot of hard-working people, some of them moviewriters, don't make that much in a whole year, sometimes in two years, or even in three or four. Do it if it won't take up too much of your time. It certainly can't do you any harm."

I like to speak to members of my family about anything of that kind that's on my mind, and so I told them about it, and we thought about it for a number of days, and finally we all decided I would hire out again.

That made it eighty thousand dollars earned in 1959. It's probably a lot of money, but if there *is* a lot, I need a lot, and frequently I need a lot when there isn't a lot. I mean, I have obligations to meet, and I myself have got to live while I am hiring out and earning money, and everything costs more than it used to. I certainly didn't gamble away every penny of the eighty thousand dollars before I went to Russia three months ago. I drank some of it away, and I bought a raincoat.

39   The Recognition

I have no quarrel with the Tax Collector, or with
the government, or with the tax laws, or with the
people who manage money better than I do. (They
may not manage other and possibly more important
things even as *well* as I do.) Or with the people who are
always getting in my way suddenly in the most stupid
manner. I have no quarrel with any other human being
in the world. But I *am* estranged from everybody, as if
I *did* have a quarrel, and of course that's also what this
is all about.

I took this flat because in order to work at all I have
got to have a little space around me, so that I can get
up from my chair any time I want to and walk around.
And the place has this terrace overlooking Taitbout and
Chateaudun, and I have got to have an outside place
like that to go to, too. And I have got to have a place in
which to gather together the junk of my life, including
the pebbles gathered by my daughter and myself on the
beach just a little outside of Athens, called Voulyag-
meni.

The three of us were there in the summer of 1957.
The secret of Greece is water. We loved the place, and
I would be there right now if there was a movie pro-

ducer there who might give me a hack job now and then.

I paid cash for this place because money is water, or as Rexroth said to my son about the money he had made reading his poems in little bars, "Snow money, it melts in your hands."

If I don't get a place to live and work in with my money, I soon find that the money is gone anyway. That's why I bought the raincoat, too.

My son once told me, "The next chunk you get, buy a whole new wardrobe."

I said, "I don't think enough about clothes, most likely, but the fact is I prefer old clothes, and the older the better."

"I just thought you ought to stop looking like a bum Pop."

Two roars of laughter.

I was driving him down Haight Street in San Francisco in the summer of 1956, through the old neighborhoods I knew, and we were kidding around about time and the world and the nature of the human experience when all of a sudden he said, "There goes Rexroth."

Well, I'd had no idea he knew his *name*, even. I hadn't seen Rexroth in fifteen years, and I became a little annoyed with my son for being so sure a man he had seen walking in the street from a moving car was Rexroth. To prove he was mistaken, and shouldn't make such statements, I swung the car around in an illegal U-turn and drove back.

"Now, which one is the one you think is Rexroth?"

"Keep going," he said. "Keep going, keep going. *This* one."

And it *was* Rexroth.

Take it or leave it, kids can do things like that.

After visiting Rexroth for an hour we resumed our drive all over San Francisco, and I said, "All right, now, just tell me how you knew the man in the street was Kenneth Rexroth?"

"Well," he said, "I'd read a couple of his poems in a magazine and I'd seen his photograph somewhere, on the cover, maybe. *The Evergreen Review* maybe."

Well, I don't know, it made me feel great.

John O'Hara has a story about a father and his boy at a ball game somewhere in the New York area. A foul ball comes into the stand near where they're seated, and of course everybody tries to catch it. Six or seven busy hands touch it for a moment, but it gets away from all hands, and finally it's lost. Everybody goes back to watching the game. On the subway home after the game the son brings the baseball out of his back pocket and rubs it in his hands, the way a pitcher does before a pitch. The father looks at the boy, and thinks, "That's my boy."

This story is one of my favorites in all of American writing. The way that father felt is the way I felt about my boy's discovery of Rexroth, first in the magazine, and then on Haight Street in San Francisco.

When I lose at gambling I'm most afraid that he may hear about it, although he's a gambler himself.

I just don't want my son to know I'm a loser, that's all. With my daughter it's different.

One night at the Aviation Club in Paris I got drunk and lucky at the same time and ran a hundred dollars up to almost fifteen thousand, but I went right on and lost it all back. The next day, numb, dumb, dumb-founded, hung over, trembling, I asked her to go for a walk with me to the Bois. During the walk I told her what had happened, precisely *as* it had happened, and all she said was, "What do we care? We've got every-thing."

But every time I lose, I'm afraid my son may hear about it. Anybody else is all right. And, as I've said, he loves to gamble, and he gambles the way I do—all out. And who started him gambling? I did. His father did.

I began taking him to the tracks around San Fran-cisco when he couldn't count to ten. Tanforan, Bay Meadows, Golden Gate Fields, and sometimes even to the tracks at little county fairs.

At Bay Meadows one time I took his sister, too, but we didn't go in, we just climbed the steep embankment to the rail at the far turn, free of charge, and pretty soon the field of twelve racing horses bunched together came thundering nearer and nearer and my daughter, then less than three, said, "Oooh, look at that." But kids speak another language: "Oooh, looka dat."

It was absolutely beautiful: Willie Shoemaker, Ishmael Valenzuela, Johnny Longden, George Tanaguchi, Ralph Neves, they were all jockeying for position, shouting curses at one another and at their mounts, which you just don't hear when you're at the races properly. The noise, enormity, power, tension, and cursing— *dirty* cursing, I may say—got my son, and he wanted to know why all the riders were mad that way. And of course I gave him a rather full account of what was involved in a horse race, in any kind of contest, any kind of competition, any event by means of which excellence ratings are achieved.

In those days, there was something more to the world than there is now. Well, my kids were little, let's put it that way, and of course if you like your kids, if you love them from the moment they begin, you yourself begin all over again, in them, with them, and so there is something more to the world again.

At the sight and sound of the horses drawing near, I felt precisely as my daughter felt. If she had felt differently, I would have felt differently. And I knew also the hushed, almost reverent, troubling of my son about what was going on, what was *really* going on.

Who are you, if you're not your kids when they are very little, when they haven't had time enough yet to become delivered from you, and from their mother, and more freely and fully themselves, or involved in an essay at becoming an aspect of themselves they prefer over other aspects?

The flat's something like a barn, in a building that's probably two hundred years old. Edmund and Jules

Goncourt lived nearby at the height of their careers, for it is in their Journal, and I came upon it by accident soon after I moved here. Chopin and George Sand were next door for a while. But I didn't come here because this part of Paris was smart a hundred years ago, I came here because it was the only place I could find that made any sense for me at all.

I was fed up with hotels, with the George V, where the rich Americans go, with the Raphael where the choosey international set, including Americans, go, and finally with La Perouse, just behind the Raphael, where Charles de Gaulle used to go. (A reporter told me, as if I would surely sleep better in my attic room knowing that.)

In Moscow at the National Hotel I was given suite 107, and one day a Moscow reporter informed me that I was living in Lenin's rooms. Just after the revolution Lenin had spent two nights in 107 before moving across the Red Square into the Kremlin. It did nothing for me.

The flat is bleak, and I want it to stay that way. There isn't a patch of carpet on the old plank floors. There is also almost no furniture in the place. The windows have outside shutters, and so there are no blinds or curtains. The floor of the entrance hall is black and white tile, black diamonds in a line of three whole ones across and a half at each end. The white is no longer white but could be made white, most likely, if anybody wanted to insist, and I don't. The tile is broken here and there, and the designs made by the breaks may very well have won me to the place. The bed is a sofa during the day, and it's trade-name is Good Boy. There are no closets in the house, so I had to buy an armoire at the same place where I bought the sofa-bed. The store is also called Good Boy.

There are three fireplaces in the place, one to a room, marble frames and mantles. Two of them are workable, but I haven't worked them.

The other one has been bricked shut for some reason. In the dining room which I have never used as a dining room is a whole fireplace-and-stove structure, after the Scandinavian manner, but I haven't used that, either.

I've used the table at which I work, and on which I eat, using newspapers both as a tablecloth and as something to read while I eat: the sofa as a sofa, and the bed of it as a bed. I have another fold-up cabinet-bed in the adjoining room, for my daughter or my son if they happen to come along. The bed of that cabinet is made up and ready. And there is a clever cot, aluminum and nylon, which could serve as an extra bed, if needed. It weighs almost nothing, and I put it here and there and spread papers out on it for sorting or study.

The bath is hopeless, but it was even more hopeless when I moved in. There's a tub in there now with a shower attachment, but the flow of hot water is so feeble, and the place is so drafty, I take a shower only when I am ready to risk pneumonia.

I have a portable radio-phonograph, sitting on a storage box, in which I have an assortment of junk, and there is a similar box in the next room, full of more junk.

I own a cave, or cellar, in the basement, but I have only visited it. It's too far to go to put anything, excepting perhaps bottles of wine, and I don't keep a cellar. Just outside my door in the hall, I have a shelved closet in which I have stacked a lot of books and old cor-

respondence and useless extra copies of manuscripts.
It's my home. It's in Paris. It doesn't mean anything.
I'm here. I work here.

The little widow upstairs who has a teen-age son and
daughter who remind me of my son and daughter is the
concierge of the building. She comes in here once a
week for two or three hours and cleans up. She's from
Algeria, and when her son or daughter speak to her they
speak in Arabic, not French, and it's good to hear them.

On the floor just below is a business firm called Pub-
liplast: publicity, of course. On the third floor is an insurance agent, but on the second floor is the joy of the
building: a father, a mother, two daughters and a son,
perhaps nine to six in years. I have seen the father es-
corting the three kids to school any number of times,
and they look great. On the first floor lives a man and
his wife.

I don't speak French and I'm not learning. I have a
set of Assimil records but I stopped listening to them
long ago. I listen to the radio while I work, and afterwards, too. I am picking up a little of the language by
a kind of osmosis, I suppose it might be called..

There is no particular reason for me to be in France
at all, or at any rate no reason of an aesthetic order. If
there were, if there could be, I might be over on the
Left Bank someplace, but I'm not especially fond of the
people over there, and that includes the famous ones. I
don't tend to go where the artists and writers tend to
go. I tend to go away from where they tend to go. I don't
think art ought to happen away from the working people. I don't need working people around me in order to
get to work, or to find out I can't work, or don't want
to, but I prefer having them around.

The only reason I'm in Paris is the producer I've

been speaking about, but I haven't made a dime from him all year and I'm not likely to, either, or ever again.

Thus, I'm here, and my junk is here, and I've got to make do. The time has come again to work and make do.

I've got to make this place work, I've got to make it shift the imbalance slowly to balance. It is all a matter of earning money, and then holding it. I can earn it, I always have when I have had to, but so far I haven't held it, and I am trying to find out how to do that.

There *is* a way.

You have got to have an attitude which I have so far scorned.

The attitude is based upon respect for money. I have got to learn to respect money. I don't *want* to learn, but I no longer have any choice.

It's damned embarrassing, I may say. It embarrasses me to know I have been humbled by money, at last. It comes to me as a kind of betrayal of something or somebody, but of what or who precisely I don't seem to know just now. In spending money, in throwing it away, in giving it away, in losing it at gambling, I have never felt that I have betrayed myself, or anything, or anybody else. But now that I am determined, from necessity, or from hunger, or from whatever you want to call it, to learn to respect money, I feel both betrayed and betraying.

Well, I *still* haven't said anything, have I? And although I have tried to begin at that end which is the opposite of the beginning, at the fiscal end, so to say, the latest day, I have failed in that, too.

I have pointed out that I am in Paris, but the fact is I am not actually in Paris at all.

I am still in the arena in which I have always pursued

the form of my life, sought its meaning, taken after my work, and done it.

The money is not *all* gone.

There is still enough for all practical purposes—for *me*, that is to say. As soon as the Tax Collector comes up with the latest figures, there will not be enough for him, if in fact there will be any for him at all that he does not seize by means of liens.

And of course even though I have earned no new money by new works this year, my old works have earned new money, but nothing like the money my hired-out labor earned for me last year.

Now, I didn't like that money, and I didn't like the way I earned it. It was desperate money.

All work is honorable, but I didn't like hiring out, I didn't feel at home about it, and the unavoidable business connected with it. The bargaining, the disputing, drove me to drink, but I won't say it also drove me to gambling. And the fact is that nothing drove me to anything.

I have always done what I have decided I wanted to do, and when I hired out, I had decided I wanted to do that. It doesn't matter that it seemed to be urgently necessary, I could still have decided *not* to hire out, to attack the problem in another way, from another point of view. I could have decided I wanted to let the Tax Collector wait until he had to decide what *he* wanted to do. Let him go right on putting liens wherever I might have money coming. But the fact is that taxes *do* have a connection with death, with the fear of it, with the impulse to postpone or avoid it, with the need to put it back in its proper place, out of mind. In forever knowing my taxes were unpaid I also knew there is such a thing as dying, and this is an unnecessary and useless piece of knowledge for a man whose business is to participate steadily and faithfully in the common human experience, to behold and to seek to understand it, and to put a little of it into usable literary forms. Why should I ever need to feel, as I frequently have since the end of the war, since the beginning of my tax indebtedness, "If I don't get my taxes paid soon, I may *never* get them paid. I may die first." I had a Beverly Hills dentist once who was a nut about the importance of flawless occlusion and all the rest of the stuff dentists deal in—inlays, caps, bridges, partials, impartials, pontoons, catamarans. There was only one religion in the world as far as he was concerned—teeth. And like most dentists he had very good teeth. By *nature* he had them, whereas by nature I had poor teeth.

One day it was necessary at last to say, "Doc, teeth are very important, I know, for chewing food, for talking, and for flashing smiles, but staying alive is also important, and this prolonged dentistry is killing me. I've been coming and going for a year, my jaws hurt, my gums hurt, the teeth with inlays in them don't feel right, and when I first started here the theory was that you would do everything I needed in under six weeks, two visits a week. Now, I know you're doing beautiful work, because you've told me so, but this is a form of beauty I can't really use. I want my mouth to begin to feel free again, and for a year it has felt caught and tortured, and not really *my* mouth, but yours. It isn't going to do at all for you to get a perfect reconstruction job in there, and then to go to my funeral." He said I was an awful kidder, but I finally had to quit and let my mouth go back to being mine—no bridges, no nothing.

Teeth, taxes, and death have something in common, most likely. And money, I might have added.

Now, we know the money is all over the place, but I'll be damned if I'm going to try to make sense of who's got the money and what he's doing with it, and who hasn't got it and what not having it is doing to him. That's for somebody else, but probably not for the Russians, as they may theoretically imagine it is.

41   The Russians

At the Hippodrome in Moscow the gamblers were precisely the same as the gamblers at any other track anywhere in the world. The horse-player is a man who has the delusion he can get the stuff without working for it, and he can't.

I have got to remember, because it stunned me—I thought I had seen everything but I hadn't—the devoted wife at the Hippodrome weeping because her husband was captured by this fantasy, this delusion that, in spite of having lost almost every ruble they had to their name, he was going right back to bet again, and to win.

I watched her, I watched him, I watched the people around them, and there, right in front of my eyes, was a great story for Dostoyevsky, Tchekhov, Tolstoy, Gorki, or me, even. She was bawling bitterly, her plain face red with despair, wet with great tears, as if she had turned her face up to heavy rain, and he was being infuriated with her, as all horse-players are, for obstructing him, jinxing him, nagging at him, interfering with his agreement with God, with fate, but not with Karl Marx, Lenin, Stalin, or any of the others who had once and for all grasped the true significance of the role of money in the human experience. His gestures were impatient and violent, his losses had turned him mad and dirty in blood, bone, nerve, bile, mind, memory, and meaning.

I had never before seen a wife of a gambler weeping. I had seen them hopeful with their husbands, or angry and scornful, cursing them and walking away, coming back, praying for a change of luck, cursing and walking away again, but I had never seen a wife weeping, and this made me feel immediately that somebody had made an awful blunder in permitting the Hippodrome to operate, in permitting the people of Moscow to find out about gambling. It just didn't seem appropriate for Russia, that's all. And the weeping woman *was* Russia, while the violent man wasn't—he was any gambler, anywhere.

I turned away after a moment, not wanting her to notice my witnessing of her despair, grief, and shame, but after the next race I went back, and there they were, and he had lost again. Now, he was looking through his pockets for more money, while she was crying harder than ever. And there *was* no more. So what would they do *now?* And what about the kids at home? He went walking away, and she just followed him, that's all.

But the hell with trying to say anything about money. It's a killer. Those who respect it and keep it need it, it's their protection, or at any rate they think it is. It surely protects up to a point, but after that point there is no protection, the same as with the horse-player. I am no enemy of Russia, but I'm not sure Russia is going to solve the problem of the people and money, of the violent horse-player and his weeping wife.

Of course all work is honorable, but the wages for most work are too little not to drive a man berserk now and then in one dimension or another. Especially when you take into account that most work is not satisfying to the worker, that he does not get something besides his wages from doing it, that it has no real connection with him, that it is an unfortunate and unavoidable necessity, that he goes to it with no love, but as a slave. Lucky is the man who loves his work. Or perhaps I had better put it this way: the wages of a man who loves his work are greater than all of the wealth of the wealthy. They are the only true wages, the only real reward any worker can use, and they constitute the only real wealth.

And so there I was in Moscow three months ago a loser still losing, both unwilling and unable to work, even though I am among the few who are lucky in that they love their work.

Well, boys, what do we do? What do we do wrong? Where do we go wrong? What do we have, what do we need, and what do we want?

Well, my Witness witnesseth, I *wanted* what I got, and what I have, including the everlasting debt to the Tax Collector. Most of all, though, I wanted to found a family, and I did, and it doesn't matter that it wasn't for long, because when you found a family, when you see the faces and hear the voices of your kids, you have found a family forever. I am a father by nature, and I need all the kids I can be a father to, or try to be a father to, for no father ever actually makes it. This is a world of sons and daughters. This is an experience for kids alone. "Absalom," he said, for he couldn't understand it. His son wanted to take his place, and his son was killed for it. What *is* his son's place? Is it the place of the father, the one who loves the mother? Is *that* the place the son wants to take away from his father, whether he knows it or not? Partly, of course. If she isn't his girl, who is? He's *of* her, isn't he, even more than he is of him, and differently.

And what is the place of the father? Is it the place of authority? Is the father the law, the guardian, the protector, the teacher? Haphazardly, willy-nilly, inaccurately, inefficiently, cruelly, stupidly, pompously, and so on? Of course. And why shouldn't the son want to take *that* place, too? If *he* doesn't, who will?

And what was *my* place as a father? My place as a father was as a *son* of both my son and my daughter. I was the one who loved the mother, but they loved her more, and differently. I was the law, but I took my instructions in the law from them.

42   The Playwright

In the morning I get up early, sometimes very early, sometimes before daylight, almost in the middle of the night. That is the true way of my life. The untrue way is for me to come home and get to bed in the morning, to be asleep when it is time to be up and at work.

As a young writer this advice came to me from somewhere: "Write, and be damned. Write, and let the form be damned. Don't imagine you are to write with your intelligence, because either you have it or you don't, and when you *do* have it, it is always in the feet, not in the head, always in the hands, always in the whole body, not in the mind. Intelligence is a much misunderstood thing. It is not the thing writers write with, so write, and don't expect to be intelligent, too. Don't expect to write with intelligence, just write, and don't expect to write one way and not another, any way will do, or if you can't do that, go back to other work, go back to a job in an office, a factory, a store, or wherever you imagine you will have a chance."

From the beginning I got up early in the morning, and I wrote. I began with poems, and I moved along to stories and plays. I wrote all kinds of plays, and every one of them was without emotionality, because emotionality seemed phoney to me.

To dispense with emotionality is the basic requirement of art in our time, which as you know is a special time, a time which simply no longer permits ranting and raving in any dimension. We shall always *have* ranting and raving of course, because it just isn't easy for this creature not to flip now and then. We shall always have emotionality, or to put it more accurately personality-sickness, the misery of selfness, of foolishness, fear, futility, falseness, fantasy, fame, and six or seven other conditions which in the English language begin with the letter F for some reason.

It is folly for emotionality to be prolonged as a means by which to achieve drama or dramatic effects in real or in artful human experience, in the world, or in the theatre, in actual events or in artful events, in human relations or in plays.

This truth is not going to be seized upon by enormous numbers of playwrights in anything like a hurry because the usages of emotionality in playwrighting are many, attractive, and convenient. *Have them jump and holler and you've got your play.*

And the reason the playwrights are not going to kick out emotionality, as I have done, as I did from the beginning of my playwrighting, is that, apart from not yet knowing enough to do so, they are spoiled by the established theatrical pattern, and the habit of audiences.

People who go to the theatre like what they like, supposedly, and in great hordes they seem to like that which is repetitious and well known, thus and so, and thus and so, and then by God here comes the ranting and the raving, here comes the acting.

And of course the playwright is bullied all over the

place by the people who take to the stage, the men and women who for some reason or another become actors and actresses, and insist upon having parts, big parts, juicy parts, easy parts, and *get* them, or else. Either the playwright rewrites a play to suit the big players, or he has no players who can draw a crowd. And a playwright *wants* to draw a crowd, and any kind of a crowd with a willingness to spend money will do.

Well, it won't do. But this does not mean the collapse of the theatre, which is in fact no more collapsible than the human personality, while the crowd, the mob, the horde, is always collapsible, although transforming the multitude is never easy. It is neither desirable nor necessary for the achievement of success in the theatre to be easy: the achievement, that is to say, of instant acceptance of a playwright and of a play, or of a series of them, or a lifetime of them, if you like.

That is something which in the nature of things should always be difficult.

But the *writing* of a play, the making of a work of art, *should* be easy. It should be as easy as the doing of any other kind of work by any other kind of workman.

It is only the theoretic need, the compulsion, to be instantly accepted that keeps the theatre, and all literary art, far behind the rights of children, the reality of them, or to put it another way the demands of the individual in the business of putting up with an unknown amount of personal time, of putting up with one's self, and of putting up with whoever else one knows importantly or unimportantly.

Within itself a play has a right to be easy only in its achievement of effectiveness. To begin with, it has got to be itself, and not a confusion of intentions and expectations based upon the winning of the current ticket-buying horde. The more a playwright strains to win the horde, the less ease he has in the making of a work, and ease is what he needs in order to achieve effectiveness in the work itself, which if it has ease will eventually win a horde in any case, but with this difference: the quality of perceptiveness, of livingness in the horde will have been improved and extended a little, after which of course the work involved, the play, will need to be transcended, just as all of Shakespeare has long needed to be transcended. It doesn't matter that no one so far has had the combination of energy, skill, wit, and health to do so.

Now, this is all very simple stuff. It isn't complicated at all. Shakespeare's drama is achieved by means of the device of emotionality, although in the comedies the order of emotionality is unlike the order that is in the tragedies. He had his horde to satisfy and he did a good job. I do not wish to be considered patronizing to Shakespeare, but it is absolute folly to go on imagining there can be no comparable dramatic force of a new and better order of drama and theatre. Emotionality as a device, as in fact the *sole* device, for the achievement of effectiveness in playwrighting is out. It is out, whether we like it or not. It has served its purpose, and it has no purpose any longer. The kids don't want it, unless the emotionality is fantasy and farce, make-believe pure and simple, for the sheer animal fun of it.

And there *will* come a time when the horde will rejoice in much of Shakespeare as farce, as an exposure of an obsolete form of man in an obsolete procedure of putting up with himself. His scheming, betraying, killing, and dying will be acceptable only as demonstrations of folly in useless but loud and grand action.

Now, it happens that I write more plays more frequently than any other living playwright, and one play is different from the other, while each of them is directed to a human race, a horde if you like, which remains concealed behind the obsolete race which is dying of the bad habit of itself. This may *seem* nonsense, but it is not nonsense at all.

What is the purpose of human life? On the animal level it is certainly to avoid pain if possible. If it is not possible, then on the human level it is in order to put up with pain decently. On the personal level, man's purpose is to be the unique thing every man is by birth, a uniqueness which is inexhaustible, although in most individuals it is extinguished almost at the outset.

Every man is entitled to be continuously alive and in transition, changing if not for the literal better at least for the usages of *recognizing* the change itself, as long as he breathes, and by means of this livingness to find himself, everybody he knows, the world, nature, time, action, and all of his exterior and interior experience dramatic, satisfying, and good.

But isn't man a tragic creature? So what? Suppose he is? He can go right on being tragic, if he is in fact tragic, if the human experience itself is, which is certainly at least still open for a final decision, or more accurately another *temporary* decision which has the appearance of finality. Man is a fluid creature, and the human experience is fluid. In him and in his life there is no vote and no final decision. Every decision is always personal first, and then collective.

Man is an accident, but the element of the deliberate in his accidental reality is now sufficient to permit him to put up with or to seek to correct the wrongs of the accidental that is in him, and to cherish, accept, recognize, employ, extend, enlarge, improve, and thrive upon the accidental *rights* which were also born into him, the principal one of which is to continue, after which the rights are inexhaustibly varied. But he must continue. He must be there, in his accidental abiding place, himself, and he must respect his right to be there as painlessly as may be.

And the plays I write are effective. They are both funny and earnest without being pompous, pretentious, affected, or excessively ambitious (startled and startling) in themselves. They take for granted that man is (also) unastonishable by the fact of his enormity. They recognize his enormity but do not rant and rave about it.

Now, in 1943 I turned my back on Broadway, but I did not stop writing plays. I simply stopped offering my plays to the machine that was huffing and puffing in the business of getting plays on the boards in front of New Yorkers and people from out of town who had money to spend on tickets. I wrote new plays every year, I have the plays, and they *do* constitute my theatre, and they are a part of the real American theatre, and of the real world theatre, even though they have not been produced, performed, and witnessed.

Such matters are none of my business.

The plays are for the human race, and they will reach the human race.

My plays *are* the human race. And most of the plays of the other playwrights aren't. But every one of my plays is *not* the human race, for I have also been pushed around. I have permitted myself to be pushed around by the horde and the machine, and by myself as well, that portion of myself which is as real as any other portion, but in illness and in desperation, in foolish desire. All the same, even in my worst plays there is much that *is* the human race, and I don't mean the obvious one.

When I speak of the human race I speak of the *concealed* human race, the *still* concealed human race, which is trying to come out from under, as it has been trying for a million years or more. Will it come out from under in the next thousand?

Well, the answer is that it is already out in myself, and we know the slob I am, the crook, the liar, the fool, and all of the other things we want to come out from under. The habit of uselessness is strong, it persists even after the element of the accidental in one man has enabled him, or driven him, to come out from under. And that doesn't matter. We want the human race entire and whole. Man doesn't have to be suddenly something different or brand-new, entirely. Just partly, just in *addition to*. And if I have come out from under, at my best, there are surely others who have as well, by the thousands, most likely, although they may not be writers, communicators, makers of influence, setters of precedents, tellers, blabber-mouths. They may keep it to themselves, not necessarily out of selfishness or indifference, but for want of a means by which to communicate.

To oversimplify for a moment, it may be said that life stinks, the human experience stinks, every individual stinks, and having said that, from having known the truth of it, the validity of it, you begin to come out from under when you reply to this truth by saying, So what? By saying, Even so. When you know it doesn't matter, when even the toughest truth, the most seemingly final and total, is recognized as also being not anywhere near tough enough on the one hand and on the other irrelevant, and is also not final and not total.

The plays I write come from health, even though I have been sick all my life. Now, whenever I say this, as I frequently do when I am chatting with a doctor, for instance, he misunderstands, and so I expect others to misunderstand, too. I expect anybody to misunderstand, so I'll see if I can make what I mean a little clearer.

We are all of us sick all our lives, but this does not necessarily mean that mortality itself is only a form of sickness that we have all become adjusted to in varying degrees. That may be the truth, but it's an irrelevant truth.

If we are sick, it follows that there exists the opposite of this, or health, for in the order of things the law of opposites is basic. If *we* are sick, *something* isn't. Or we ourselves are also simultaneously something else, *not* sick, the opposite, healthy. If it is desirable to cease to be sick, or less sick, or at any rate to achieve a balance between the opposites, it is desirable to go after the fulfillment of this possibility. It is desirable not to make ourselves sicker than we are, and it is desirable to try to make ourselves more well than we are, without of course forfeiting the advantages of being more sick than well, which can be considerable. A man sicker than well doesn't forget, for instance, the collective pain and discomfort of everybody, and that *is* an advantage. In the matter of opposites I am on the side of more instead of less, however difficult, increasingly, more is for me to cope with. I am on the side of health instead of sickness, right instead of wrong, energy instead of disspiritedness, enjoyment instead of distaste, but more than anything else truth instead of falsity, even though I know that all truth is also inevitably false, tentative, tenuous, troublesome. But as you continue to come out from under and to stay out, you move nearer to something more and better than everything else. This state so far is not even *named,* not even by a sign or symbol in mathematics, or in some other form of science. You move nearer to what I shall mistakenly call the Intelligence-of-All, even though I know it is not intelligence, and that nothing we are able to conceive may be said to be All. Having come out and being out, you get it entirely, not with mind alone, not with nerves alone, flesh and blood and chemistry and the action of it all in concert alone, you get it entirely, and you get it out, *away* from yourself above all things, and yet inevitably always yourself, too, for you are the one there, moving and transitory. And you can't say that it is *knowing,* either, although it is certainly something of that order. Perhaps it might (also) be said that it is a state of being in which by having become most yourself, which at most is a picayune fragment of the possible total, you have also ceased to be so uselessly yourself alone, and have become delivered from this smallness and uselessness into the vicinity, if vicinity can even suggest it, of unself, or multitudiness, which all the same is you, is yours.

This involvement in an apparent contradictoriness is also unavoidable. The more you are yourself, the fuller you are yourself, the greater the range and variety of the action and elements of yourself, the less you are yourself as formerly.

I write my plays out of that kind of health, and it is important to me to do so, to write them, to have written them. And the writing of them has nothing to do with Broadway, with the preferences of the current horde, with theatre buildings, with the machinery of production, with real estate, with money, with acceptance, with instant material profit.

But how can that possibly be?

Haven't I already made known that nobody is more ambitious than I am, more compelled to be instantly accepted, more willing to fit his work to the habit of uselessness?

So what?

I'm a gambler. I want a lot of money, so I can throw it around, as a demonstration of something or other.

Surely what I'm saying is some kind of self-deception, isn't it? Possibly, but that does not matter either, because of *what* I am trying for, and *how* I am trying, and the fact that I have lived only fifty-two years, and it hasn't been enough.

To sum up, I am great, and I am proud to be great. It is quite a responsibility. I might have been a car thief.

43   The Letter

A writer is always writing, even when he only thinks
and feels the writing, and doesn't get it on paper: poems,
stories, plays, declarations, testimony, and letters such
as this one:

Dear Mr. Suit: I have your letter dated yesterday, so
I presume it was dictated to your secretary sometime
yesterday and that consequently you are still alive and
kicking.

In the letter you are kicking about the unfair terms I
have suggested in answer to the unfair terms you suggested last week in the matter of a play I wrote about
two people on a desert island that turned out to have a
fashionable hotel on it, which the man found out but
concealed from the woman, and the woman found out
and concealed from the man. This idea was not my own.

It was an idea from a writer I don't know, and when
you told me the idea you said, "Now, if you would write
a play like that, I could make you rich."

I said I could write a play about anything, but what
about the other writer?

You said, "Leave that to me."

While I was writing the play you wrote a letter in

which you suggested the unfair terms I have just referred to, and I answered the letter. You wrote again,
and you telephoned two or three times, and you got rid
of some of the unfairness of your terms, and I handed
you a copy of the finished play, so you could see how
little importance the original idea had in it. Two people
on a desert island has been the subject of jokes, cartoons,
stories, novels, and plays for at least a thousand years.
But still you felt the original idea, as you put it, was in
fact original, and the most important element in the
play.

Again I replied: "Now, you know I wrote this thing
for money, and your business is money. All the same in
view of the time and energy I was wasting talking and
writing about this matter to you, I told you there was
one sensible solution to the problem. I would put the
play away. You would hand back to the other writer his
original idea, and everything would be as it had been
before you made known to me that you believed if I
would write such a play you could make me rich. Now,
the fact is I *am* rich. In short, no deal, and let's not
waste any more of my time, as I am trying to write a
poem."

You wrote again and said, "All right, all right, I have
solved the problem, don't ask me how, and all I want is
ten percent of the income from the play, from all
sources, for the term of the copyright, which is around
thirty-seven years, I understand."

Now, you appear to be a man of sixty, although you
may be younger, and I appear to be a man of sixty-six,
although I am actually fifty-two. In thirty-seven years
you will be ninety-seven years old, and I presume in excellent health, at your desk in your office on the Champs-
Elysees every morning promptly at half past five, as I

understand the oldest men don't like to sleep in the morning. The year will be 1997, and the play will be out there bringing in the shekels, as we used to say in Fresno. I will be eighty-nine, and much interviewed by young newspapermen who by that time will be thinking of me as one of the greatest writers of all time.

I suggested, nevertheless, that if you could make a big deal on behalf of the play within three months, O.K.

If you are waiting for money, if you are waiting to get rich, as I am, three months is a long time. And I suggested that having thirty-seven years in which to get me rich could not be considered swift action for a businessman. It might be considered swift enough for a writer, because making big deals and getting rich isn't a writer's speciality.

Now, you have just come back with another letter: "I have reread your letter several times and I am still a little confused. I ask myself whether the man who writes such delightful plays is the same man who writes such letters of no delight."

I herewith reply in the affirmative: "They are one and the same."

And then you say, "Indeed the play is charmingly written and very amusing and I am sure (knock on wood) that it will have the success it well deserves."

That did it. Charmingly written, very amusing, knock on wood.

Am I going to have to put up with talk like that in 1997, with a new century on the verge of dawning at last? The very thought terrifies me.

But there is still more, and I wish there weren't: "Generally speaking, writers should not make deals. This is especially true for you, if for no other reason than your tax situation. I could help you with this most constructively and I would like to explain to you orally, how."

My friend, I *know* how: by having enough money to pay off the Tax Collector in full. Any explanation you make, orally, or in any other manner, cannot change that fact. And that's what this is all about. I want money, and you want thirty-seven years, two different things. You're welcome to the thirty-seven years, but that is a matter between you and others.

As for me, I don't believe I want to know you in 1997.

My best to you always, and remember me to Mrs. Suit.

I write a letter, without ever putting it into words, something like the foregoing letter, every day.

I have been writing such letters since I bought the upright Underwood in 1921, in Fresno. I used to write them on the typewriter and mail them, but nobody appreciated them, so I stopped mailing them, and finally I stopped writing them, too. I didn't *think* them, either. They just happened while other things were happening, while I was working on the writing of a new story or play, for instance. They just moved along on their own, while I moved along on my own. The provoking letter, or party, or condition, was finally actually answered, but not in anything like the manner I have just described. The actual answer was something like this, as a rule: "O.K." This appears to be the direct opposite of the unwritten answer, both as to length and as to meaning, but I doubt very much if it *is* the opposite, or that Mr. Suit will actually outlive the copyright, or that the play will make me rich.

A man of letters ought to write letters, too, that's all. The difficulty is in finding people to write them to. My own favorites have always been God, members of the family, especially my own kids, and lawyers, because when you write to lawyers things have gone so far that you have got to write a letter of enormous insignificance. The answering of letters from the Tax Collector is also an interesting activity, and most of these are not written, although a few are. The Tax Collector's letters are invariably mimeographed and all they say is that you still haven't paid him. Sometimes the print is so faded it can barely be made out, and the scribbled signature is *never* legible. It always looks something like Jvgtl, which of course is nobody.

44   The Egg

I sometimes *actually* answer kids in English classes, however, who want to know the real meaning of something in *The Human Comedy*.

For instance, Ulysses goes running home from the railroad track where he waved to a singing Negro riding a freight train. The man not only waved back to him, which the engineer had not done, but also called out to him. Ulysses runs straight to the chicken coop in the yard of his house, and to the laying nest there, where he finds one egg. He picks up the egg and runs to his mother, who is hanging clothes on the line in the yard, and he looks at her but doesn't say anything. He just hands her the egg. Well, now, the whole class talked about that for some time, and so on behalf of the class Ava Gardner (yes, she has the same name as the movie actress but doesn't want a career in the movies, only wants to be as intelligent as possible and some day be a good wife and mother) sends a letter to the writer, and the letter is forwarded to three old addresses and finally reaches the writer in Paris.

Ava wants to know, "What did Ulysses mean by handing his mother that egg?"

Dear Ava Gardner: Thank you very much for your kind letter, which I am sorry to say wandered around for six weeks, so that I am only now able to try to answer it, when it's too late for the writing of the term papers for your English class at Lincoln High School in Fargo, North Dakota.

To begin with, I think you ought to know that a writer may not know what something he has written means, although this doesn't necessarily mean that it doesn't mean anything.

The obvious meaning of course is that a boy of three or four, speechless with gladness because a total stranger, traveling away, saw him, answered his wave, and called out to him in the voice of a friend, again has found an egg in the nest where miraculously eggs keep appearing. Now, an egg is white, it is whole, and the shape of it is quite startling in its simplicity and flawlessness. An egg is good to see. To some people it is as good to see, again and again, as a great work of sculpture, for it is in fact the greatest of such works, the first of them, and of course we know an egg is not shaped by a sculptor, it is laid by a hen. Or at any rate the egg that the little boy found *was*. At his age he may not have known that. He may not have suspected any connection between the ten or eleven hens and the one rooster and the appearance of eggs in the laying nest. He may not have known at all how the eggs got there. He may only have known that if he went to the nest often enough he would see an egg, and he liked going, and he liked seeing an egg. The same thing, almost, every time, but each egg is a new egg, each egg is itself. He may even have believed that his going *made* each egg, that an egg was out there as a reward to him for being alive, for being interested in everything, for not understanding very much, and for many other reasons which only little children know.

Now, of course, little children don't know very many

words, they're not very good at language, they don't
know how to say what they feel and believe and know,
or think they know, as the rest of us do. Having greeted
the traveler, who was going home, far away, and having
become filled with a mixture of gladness and solemnity,
and a little loneliness, by the sight and sound and gesture of the traveler, and by his warmth and understanding and swift friendship, Ulysses may have felt that now,
for sure, he would be rewarded with an egg, a new egg,
the egg of the mixture, of having been seen by a total
stranger, a big man with a big voice and a dark skin, of
having been astonished by the man's swift acceptance of
him, a small boy standing among weeds watching another train go by, of feeling suddenly a part of the
traveler, a part of all travelers, of all strangers, of the
whole human race. He may have felt that he would find
the egg of many meanings, the egg perhaps of all meanings, the gathering together in one small white real
thing that you could pick up with your hand and look
at, a gathering together into a perfect form of all mute
truth, the truth of the eye, which all creatures have, but
children most of all.

And the egg *was* there, and Ulysses was there, and the
traveler was gone. Ulysses may have felt a touch of loneliness, not for members of his family alone when he was
away from them, or for people he had met and known
enough to like and had thought about ever since, but
for any people, all people, going, gone, and perhaps
never to be seen again. And his mother was there, and
of course every man's mother *is* his mother, a wonderful
and astonishing gift, but his father *wasn't* there, his
father was gone, perhaps he had gone as the traveler on
the freight train had gone, and the boy may have felt a
renewal of his longing to see his father because of his

separation from the traveler. He didn't understand about death, he didn't know he would never see his father again, and he took the egg to his mother, and looked at her again, at the marvel and miracle of her, and for all I know, Ava, in handing her the egg he meant that he hoped the traveler would get safely home, that his own father would come walking down the street soon and be home again, and that he loved his mother, he loved his father, he loved his brothers and his sisters, and the traveler, and the whole strange business of being himself, named Ulysses, in the world, a part of it now and forever, and a part of all of the people in it.

But he didn't know how to say so much. Perhaps the egg would say it for him.

Is it possible that *that* might be something like what Ulysses meant by handing his mother the egg?

I don't know, because I certainly didn't *say* what he meant. I said he meant all the things he couldn't say. I suppose I let it go at that because I imagined the reader would remember having done pretty much the same thing and would get the idea, and perhaps even by then *know* pretty much what Ulysses meant. It means anything, Ava. Anything means anything. You will decide for yourself what anything means. It's really up to you entirely. The more you can make something mean the better.

But if the letter is from a teacher of English, I tell her I hope she isn't using my book to give the kids a bad time with, because I am opposed to giving kids a bad time. I am in favor of giving them a good time, always.

45   The Papers

And then there are letters from the Library of Congress asking if I have made provisions to place my papers on deposit somewhere appropriate, and how about the Manuscript Division of the Library of Congress?

Well, my father's papers were placed on deposit inside a laundered and ironed flour sack, and hauled around from place to place and carefully kept by my mother, and I saw them, I examined them, and doing so was one of the great events of my life, so there can be no question about the importance of having the papers on deposit somewhere, but of course the copyright on the new play doesn't run out until 1997, and I don't want to run out until then, either.

And there is always the question, Who are the papers on deposit *for?*

My idea about this is that I would like to carry on the tradition established by my father and leave my papers to my son and to my daughter, and to their sons and daughters, but then there is always the chance that they may not be interested. They may not have time for so many papers. In fact it is inconceivable that they could possibly have time enough to examine the original manuscripts of works that have been published, let alone the stuff that hasn't been published and will not have been published by 1997, even. By that time my son will be fifty-four, two years older than I am now, and my daughter will be precisely my age now. They may not be interested in writing at all, and looking at a lot of old manuscripts, published or not, isn't likely to have very much appeal for them.

So who do I leave the papers on deposit for, and where? By God, I just don't like the idea of leaving them anywhere.

All the same, I've got to decide where they are to stay, and who they are to stay for.

The Manuscript Division of the Library of Congress could very well be as sensible a place as any, but I would like to visit the place first and find out how it works. If the people who run the place tend to be rude to people who come in looking like bums, I don't want my papers to be left there. A lot of the finest minds and spirits look like bums, and I am opposed to giving bums the bum's rush. I've been given that rush in very nearly every official place I have ever tried to visit and use. Only the public libraries have been indifferent about my appearance, although I have had some bad times with some of the older employees, who are a lot like school teachers. "We shall look forward to hearing from you, and hope that the first installment of the Saroyan papers will shortly be on its way to the Library." Well, the letter was written only two weeks ago, and received only two days ago, so perhaps there's no rush.

Dear Library: I want my papers until 1997. Please write to me at that time, and if it looks as if I'm not going to see the dawning of the next century, I will try to reach a decision and to reply promptly to your letter, one way or the other. As matters stand, the papers I have accumulated so far are all over the world. New stuff is added to the old every year, and sometimes there is a lot of it. Most of it is written and never looked at again. There was a time, most likely, when I meant to examine stuff written and not published, but there was suddenly too much of it and I was always too busy writing new stuff to bother. There are at least ten million words of unpublished stuff already on hand here and there, and some day perhaps a specialist of some kind will run through the stuff, or a little of it, and pick out a few words on the subject of gambling, for instance, but already I feel sorry for him, because he would do better to go and gamble and find out for himself. And if he happens to be a biographer, I feel very sorry for him, because so much of my stuff that's unpublished is in plain English, and so much of it is dead-pan spoofing (of myself, of the illusion of myself, that is, of the non-myself myself, so to say). But the whole thing gets even more complicated when I point out that sometimes the spoofer is the non-myself myself, while the spoofed is myself. For instance, let's say I write, "I am the stupidest man in the world. I have proven it again by having just finished a new play which is great. It is stupid to write a great play. The brilliant thing to do, the intelligent thing to do, always, is to go out into the world and live like a Lord— well dressed, money in the pocket, a beautiful girl on the arm, the best food, the best drink, unimportant but pleasant talk, laughter, jokes, fun, love, health, and the sport of a man with a woman. What do I want with another great play?" And so on. Well, who spoofed and who *was* spoofed? In any case, whoever undertakes to mess with my papers has got his work cut out for him. It can be done. Anything can be done. A fair biography *might* be cooked up from the papers. It might read all right, but it won't be a biography of me, because there is no such thing, of anybody. It will be the writing of the writer of the biography, as Pearson's Shaw is Pearson, not Shaw, and even as Shaw's Shaw in Pearson's biography is also not Shaw but Pearson's Shaw's Shaw, which is another thing entirely. And Shaw's own Shaw is not Shaw, either. What the hell does *he* know about Shaw?

But I'm thinking about it, Library.

And then there is a letter from the Department of State: "We have reservations concerning the accuracy of statements attributed to you by the *Moscow Literary Gazette* of September 29, 1960. A thermofax copy of the article and of the Soviet translation thereof are enclosed." That's all.

Dear Passport Office, Department of State: I have read your letter and I have examined the two enclosures. From the letter I can't make out whether I am expected to reply, but at the same time I also can't decide why the letter and the enclosures were sent to me if a reply was not expected. Or is it possible I just don't understand the language employed by the various departments of the government? Is it possible, that is to say, the letter actually says very clearly that I had better reply, or else? That is to say, what is the connection between the Passport Office and my having recently been in Russia? I'm used to saying what I mean, or at any rate I'm used to *trying* to say what I mean. And I'm not used to trying to make out meanings which aren't said at all.

Is this, then, what is known as a veiled threat?

Well, if it is, I suppose it's all right for a veiled threat to be directed to me. I suppose it's all right for me to be expected to unveil it, and if that's so, I'll try. If it's the least I can do, it's also the most I can do, as far as I can judge from where I sit. I sit here in this ice-cold barn of a flat in Paris, on a very cold and drizzly day in mid-November, and it's nearly like night, although the time is only half-past one in the afternoon.

First, perhaps, we ought to take up who I am, in case that is in order.

I am a poet. I write poetry in English in the form of short stories, novels, and plays, as a rule, although sometimes I actually write a poem, or try to, and I write poetry in other forms than the three I have mentioned. Now, a poet is required to take out a passport the same as anybody else, and when he travels he is required to pay his fare the same as anybody else. A poet travels for any number of reasons, including the basic reason of all true travelers: to go. To be going, to arrive, to be there, to go on, to have been there, to remember having been there. The poet also travels because his poetry comes from the world and the people and he needs to see as much of them as possible.

Now, you must know, or at any rate suspect, Mr. Passport Office, that a poet, like a scientist, is obsessed by the truth, by the hope of achieving a little more of it than ever before, even though he knows any achievement of it must finally turn out to have been temporary. Still, it is better than nothing. A poet tries to live truthfully, no matter what the actual events of his life may be, and he tries to think and feel truthfully, and above all things to speak and write truthfully. Speaking and writing are, as you know, forms of the same thing: communicating, making contact. A poet can't speak untruthfully and expect to write truthfully. He's got to *breathe* truthfully,

even. And of course you may also know that it is an
established procedure almost everywhere in the world
for newspapermen to present themselves to visitors, including poets, and to ask them questions. It happens to
me all the time, everywhere I go: Japan, Australia, England, France, Italy, Spain, and so of course it happens in
Russia, too. The newspapermen and women ask questions and I answer them. Being the same man wherever
I go, I answer the questions in one place precisely as I
do in another—that is, as truthfully as I know how, as
unimportantly as possible in order to avoid the embarrassment of feeling pompous, as pleasantly as may be,
with as much respect as possible for the asker of the
questions. And you may also know that newspapermen
are either not very good writers, or they all use the answers they hear in any way that they believe will make
their story, their interview, most interesting for the readers of the paper they write for. They never quote
entirely accurately. Sometimes they actually invent
stuff.

The most popular newsweekly of the United States,
for instance, has made it traditional for all of its writers
to distort, to twist, to put fresh emphasis upon, and even
to rewrite most of the answers they hear. This has happened to me many times. The questions were *Time*
Magazine questions, but still they were answered in the
only manner of answering questions that I have, which
I have already described. Had you read any of the remarks attributed to me by *Time,* I hope you would have
had reservations about them, just as you have reservations about the remarks (your word is statements) attributed to me by the *Gazette* in Moscow. If you did,
you certainly didn't write and tell me. And that is how
it was with respect to my remarks, or statements, in

Honolulu, Tokyo, Hong Kong, Singapore, Bombay, Cairo, Athens, Rome, Paris, London, Melbourne, Sydney, Madrid, and a number of other cities.

I was misquoted, and nobody noticed.

But now I have been misquoted in Moscow, and somebody has noticed. You, Mr. Passport Office. And you have called to my attention that I appear to have been misquoted, and you have sent me a thermofax copy of the interview in the Russian language, which I do not read, as well as a translation into English, which I do.

I examined the thermofax copy of the interview that is in the Russian language, and it has every appearance of being an interview. It is probably an interview *with me* because there is a drawing of me in the second of the four columns of the interview, and I remember the man sitting in the editorial office of the *Literary Gazette*, making the drawing. For about an hour I chatted with five men and two women, all of whom wrote for that paper, or helped get it out. I was interested in those people, and in their paper. And so we know I was there and something was written about my having been there, and it was published in the paper. And you have noticed it and you have let me know that you have noticed it. And of course I must wonder why, since it has never happened before. And so I must examine the translation of the interview, to see if I can get a clue from *that*.

Quote. "You say you want to know what I think about the dynamics of Soviet development?" Saroyan asked and added with a smile: "Oh, I am a 'great expert' on politics and economics. But joking apart, every time I come to the Soviet Union I see truly incredible changes for the better. One cannot but feel respect for these tremendous achievements and changes. And I think that in the coming ten years your successes will be still greater than in all of the forty odd hard years past. America cannot help noticing these changes and no wonder it fears that Russia will overtake it." Unquote.

There is so much more of this same dull order of writing that perhaps I might be permitted to skip some of it, and see if I can get to the worst.

Quote. "The meaning of the word 'win' has now changed. We must live in peace. We must argue and compete but without the sword. The Russians teach patience and we must really be patient—for five or ten years—because nowadays war is suicide. *And far from all want to be suicides.*" Unquote.

Well, now, the last sentence I just can't figure out at all. Did the Russians have a sentence that meant something? Did the translator leave something out? I don't know.

And I can't be bothered with any more that is in the interview, because it's of the same order. And it just isn't my kind of order. I can't read stuff like that. But let's get to the point. Suppose I *had* said everything that is in the interview? Would you want me to write and tell you, "Relax, Mr. Passport Department. I am a patriot. I love America and I hate Russia."

Well, I won't do that. If you were to expect such a reply from me, which you may very well do, I would have to consider your expectation an insult. It is not necessary for me to feel I have been, am being, or shall be, insulted, and then to feel that I must nullify the insult, either by insulting right back, or by being compelled to state that which I take for granted. And so I can't do that, either. I refuse to do it. I am not employed by the government, or by any branch of it. I have never been so employed. I was drafted into the Army during the War for a period of three years during which I was obliged to take orders, but that war has long since been over. I pay my way wherever I go, and I speak for myself. I wouldn't know how to speak for anybody else. If your message is asking me *not* to speak, even for myself, I am sorry, I cannot accept any such instruction. If your message is asking me to watch it when I speak, especially when I am in those parts of the world which are presently identified by the government, or individuals in it, as the Enemy, again I am sorry, I cannot accept that suggestion, instruction, or threat, either. I remember when the Enemy was Germany, Japan, and Italy, each of which is now the Friend. I don't consider people in terms of friend or enemy. I consider them only in terms of themselves, as people. I make no friends and I make no enemies. I make a lot of acquaintances. Are you sure, Mr. Passport Office, that some day it is not going to be the policy of the government to identify Russia as the Friend and somebody else as the Enemy, perhaps somebody who is now identified as the Friend? I know it isn't easy to be a government, and insofar as you are a government, you have my sympathy. It's hard enough to be a poet.

But then of course there is no end to the letters I write and don't send, or the letters I think and don't write. I could never even begin to suggest the range of them.

47   The Place

The year 1960 has a silly unreal look to it. The line-up of the numbers seems unfortunate, and one must be sympathetic toward anybody born in such a year.

Next year will be different, though: the numbers will have a proper look to them: 1961, the two ones at each end making it something from which to derive comfort and to expect miracles. The interior nine and six are virtually flawless. How I envy the man born in 1961. He should have a good life.

November is one of the better months. It has dignity, and a quality of sobriety and resignation.

Time has done its worst, the other months of the year have come and gone, wreaking havoc, as the saying is, but a man is still there, moving through November to December, to the last day of an unfortunate but unavoidable year.

The Paris of the Opera-Trinity-St. Lazare-Notre Dame de Loret area is a pleasant Paris.

Rue Taitbout is in honor of Sam Taitbout, the vegetarian veterinary, who was killed in a duel over a dog when he refused to run through his opponent. He knew Archie Crashcup, Archie Minasia, and Archie Toke, three of the best, but in the end it didn't help. The number is 74.

Number 74 came to this building in the usual order of numbers, following closely on the heels of 72.

The floor is the fifth.

The room is the main room, but I wouldn't care to call it the drawing room. It is simply the first room to the left as you come in the door, although I have made all of my drawings here.

In this room is the sofa-bed, now made up and looking for all the world as if it were in fact a comfortable sofa covered with a green-black coarsely woven material of some kind.

It is directly in front of the work table, along the wall in a rather clever place, if I do say so myself.

Directly opposite the sofa, and behind the chair in which the writer sits, is the fireplace, lately rendered nil but still of good appearance, classicly designed in gray marble with black streaks, lightly here, and heavily there.

Over the fireplace, is a large mirror with a golden frame, and on the mantle of the fireplace is a row of books, a stack of phonograph records, a box flashlight, a transistor radio, three pocket knives, a small yellow ashtray from a Paris hotel, and a clever pair of opera glasses which are also a compass, a magnifying glass, and one or two other things, bought for a dollar from a street hawker whose style of oratory I admired, although I could not understand anything he said, or the meaning of his pointed finger to this, to this, and to this. Its frame is gray plastic and it fits, shut, into a transparent plastic case. Four ballpoint pens, two found, two given by confused travel agents. A quince from Armenia turning black with spots. A bottle of American ink, cigarettes, matches in boxes, and three clean sculptural bones from an ox-tail, which I have begun to study.

And finally there is a smart-looking electric lamp on the mantle.

To the left of this desk, in the corner of the room, is a gray French filing cabinet, on top of which are miscellaneous manuscripts, answered mail, and another quince, entirely gone but still stinking up the place, as I want it to do: decay and deterioration must also be noticed with respect.

Besides the filing cabinet is the first of two old-fashioned window-doors which lead to the terrace. Between the two window-doors is a plain, strong wooden box, about three feet in length and two and a half in depth and width, with black stenciling: *65 TRANSPORTS GUERIN PARIS*.

On the box is an open portable radio-phonograph, Victor, His Master's Voice, and the radio is going.

On one side of the box is another stack of records, the ones I am using at the present time: Mozart Concerto No. 20 en re mineur K. 466, Orchestre Symphonique de Vienna, Clara Haskil, piano. I sought this one out, as I wrote by it more than ten years ago, in San Francisco, when Arthur Schnabel was at the piano. I believe he did it better than Miss Haskil, although a concert pianist at a party not long ago informed me that she did it closest to the way he had done it. Schnabel died.

The other L.P. is an album bought by my son, unaccountably, last year: *The Lively Guy,* with a big smiling photograph of Guy Lombardo. I gave my son a bad time for throwing his money away on music of that kind, but I wish I hadn't, because I have come to cherish the songs played and the choruses sung, not because I miss my son and he bought the disc for me, but because the songs remind me of old times.

The most important record I have, though, is a simple

old-fashioned record of 78 RPMs, given as a gift by the singer of the song, inscribed by him in Armenian which I can't read: Hovsep Badalyan, and brought by me from Erivan to Paris. While driving out to Burakan, to meet Viktor Ambartsoumian, the astrophysicist, I first heard the song on the car radio, and was so moved by it, I asked what it meant, and who was singing. I have already remarked how important I consider songs, and how much they have always meant to me, and how much they mean now. The name of the song is *Horovel*. It is the *Plowman's Song*. The animal drawing the plow is the ox, or as it is put in Armenian, *yez*. It's a people's song. Nobody wrote it. The people made it up, at work. It is a chant, a call, to earth and animal. The plowman calls the ox his heart-brother. A great song. In Erivan the singer of the song was brought to my hotel one night, and there he sang the song, as a dozen of us listened and drank, and joined him in singing it. In Paris I listen to this disc most of all, because it is mine, out of my family, out of my olden earth.

When I was seventeen the songs of Armenia, sung on discs by Armenak Shah-Mouradian of Moush, became profoundly important in my life. I played them on the phonograph and sang them with the great singer. Hearing his singing for the first time I thought, "So *that's* what it is to be an Armenian. That open-voice, field-voice, wind-voice, voice of the plains."

In front of the stack of records on the box is a black telephone, at the end of the longest cord I have ever seen. The cord, the phone, and the number, came with the place. I made a small effort to get a new phone and cord, but I ran into a French-style argument, so I let it go. I don't use a phone that much, and anybody's phone might as well be my phone, too.

Along the wall to the right is the armoire, or closet: seven feet high, four doors, and in the armoire hang my old clothes, or lie on shelves, and that's it, that brings me back to the work table, which has a black metal base, a pitch-black surface made of something that has a name that I can't remember, and just beyond this black stuff, to the right, are two drawers of blond wood.

The chair has black legs and six slim black back sticks in the part that goes up from the seat.

On the seat is the writer, and that's who I am, at home, at work.

I can think of nowhere else I would rather be or anything else I would rather be doing. I am here, and I am who I am.

Perhaps you know where you are, and who you are.

48   The Time

The year 1959 started in Malibu, with the closing of a
house on the beach, after six years.

The pain of packing the old manuscripts, books,
and papers was great. The stuff was hauled off and put
in storage, and I hauled off and left that place forever.

From the beginning I had thought of the place as
heaven, as perhaps it was, but even heaven will not do,
cannot do, forever. It must be closed, and the back must
be turned to it.

I went to New York, but it was not for me.

I went to Belgrade, but it was not for me.

I bought a Red Racer, and I raced. To Trieste, Venice, Milan, Geneva, Aix-en-Provence, Nice, San Remo,
Monte Carlo, Cannes, and finally up to Paris, where I
wrote a play for money, as I've said, rented an apartment
on Avenue Victor Hugo, to which my kids flew from
New York.

For three and a half months we were together, and
then they were gone, and I was back in a hotel room. I
drove the Red Racer to Spain and back, and then I took
a ship from Genoa to Australia.

In the rented apartment on Avenue Victor Hugo I

wrote a book called *Not Dying*. On the ship to Australia I wrote a book called *Joey in the Pouch*. In the apartment I also wrote a play called *Nobody in His Right Mind, or The Moscow Comedy*, and on the ship I also wrote a play called *Kangaroo and Boomerang*. And that was 1959.

From Malibu in 1958 I went around the world, taking with me the daily work of writing *Fifty Fifty*, started on the first day of my fiftieth year, September 1, 1957, finished on the last, August 31, 1958, as planned. A million words, give or take a couple of thousand. Too many, too long, and I wasn't interested in revising it, in finding out what I had, so it went into storage with the rest of my junk.

My kids came out to California from New York that summer, and mainly we had a lot of fun, but one thing happened that was no fun.

We drove up to San Francisco to spend a couple of weeks at my sister's home, and then we drove back to Malibu, by way of Fresno, and as we were driving around among the vincyards near Malaga my son asked me to stop, so we could pick some grapes. So we could *steal* some, if you like. I stopped, and ran out into the vineyard and began picking the grapes, only to notice that my son was just standing there looking at them. I told him to start picking, but he just went right on looking.

"I don't think they're ripe," he said.

"Even so," I said, "pick a couple of bunches."

I ran back to the car. He came back, taking his time, but he didn't have a single bunch of grapes with him.

This bothered me.

He had asked me to stop, and I had stopped, and then

he hadn't done anything to make the stop worth anything.

I bawled him out about this, and about his boredom all during the drive, and then I bawled out my daughter, too. My sister said something, and I bawled her out, too, and then for an hour or more nobody spoke.

By that time I felt foolish, but at the same time I couldn't understand my son, so I asked if he had had a bowel movement in the morning.

He hadn't. And he'd had a headache all day.

I told him about myself when I had been his age. I had had nothing, but I had always been interested, fascinated even, by everything. On and on.

I knew it at the time, I know it now, and I suppose he knew it, too: I was being angry at his mother.

It was stupid, but I couldn't help it, that's all.

I stopped somewhere for an aspirin for him, but he said he believed a Coke would do him more good, so he had a Coke, as everybody did, but whatever had been going on went right on going on.

My past was kicking me around, and with it I was kicking my son around, and every now and then my daughter, a little, too.

I tried to get out of it, to get myself out of being so mad at their mother, and at them, too, but it didn't work, and so I blamed my son.

Why wasn't he livelier, more comic, more alert, so that I would be driven out of the madness?

He didn't know. All he knew, but didn't say, was that he hated me, and I couldn't blame him, but I hated being hated.

I said that my trouble had been that I had loved them too much, had tried to do too much for them, had paid too much attention to every wish they had ever had, and of course they knew I meant their mother hadn't, which I believed to be true. From now on I would be different, I said. I would be like other fathers. I would give them orders. The other fathers were right, I was mistaken. I had looked upon them from the beginning as equals, or even superiors, and now I could see the folly of that.

I talked for hours and miles, and nobody replied, nobody dared, or cared, or needed to.

Now, I must point out that such talking is traditional in my family. It is invariably loud, intense, righteous, and critical of all others.

All families probably have their own procedure for the achievement of psychiatric therapy or the restoration of balance, and the better part of this procedure is based upon talk, although it frequently moves along to shouting and fighting.

Six or seven times during the long recitation I tried to get out of the whole thing by laughing at myself, by making known that I knew I was being a fool, by saying things I believed were both true and amusing, but nobody laughed.

It was a very hot day in July, and from the beginning it had been a bad day.

In the back of the old Cadillac my daughter sat beside my sister, and beside me sat my son, drawn away on the car seat, the old Saroyan scowl all over his face.

At last the car began to climb the hills of Pacific Palisades, and soon we would be home.

I was still going strong when suddenly my son said in a tone of voice that still hurts me, and has twice come to me in my sleep: "Papa, Papa, will you stop the car, please?"

I stopped the car, he leaped out, and in the very leap

began to buckle and vomit, trying to hide behind a tree whose trunk was too narrow for hiding. The sound of his sickness sickened me. Once, twice, three times, four times, five times. Silence. His face was drained of color and covered with sweat.

Immediately after he had jumped out of the car my daughter jumped out, saying, "Aram, what's the matter? What's the matter, Aram?"

My sister said in Armenian, "You've made the poor boy sick. He isn't like you. He's like himself."

We got home, and I got him into the shower, and then into a robe, and at the table for some hot chocolate and toast and boiled eggs, and then I had them both go to bed, even though it was only beginning to be dark, and their old friends in the neighborhood were coming to the door to ask them out for games.

That's the thing that bothered me in 1958, and will go right on bothering me the rest of my life.

I only hope it isn't the last thing I remember.

He told me the next day that it hadn't been my hollering at him that had made him sick, it had been other things.

I thanked him, but I didn't believe him, because I couldn't.

And my sister had been right in saying that he wasn't like me, only she'll never know how like him I was, but never vomited, because if I had, I might not be able to stop.

And I was sorry he wasn't like me, in that, because it is better not to get sick, it is better to find out how not to, it is better to insist on it, even, until it's almost impossible to get that sick, because getting sick doesn't get it, doesn't do it, at all.

But he hurt me, he hurt me deeper even than the

failure and death of friends, and I loved him more than ever, and despised myself for never having been able to get sick that way, and for having made him sick that way, making him vomit for me forty years ago.

I went home one night from the winter streets of Fresno, possessed. Something had taken possession of me, hushed me, estranged me, put me aside from myself, and I wanted to get rid of it. The house was dark and empty when I got there, and cold, and I didn't know what to do. In the dining room was a bench my mother had made by placing planks over two apple-boxes and putting a coarse woven covering over the planks: red and black checks made out of some kind of sacking, made in Bitlis by somebody in the family. I couldn't sit and I couldn't lie down, so I kneeled on this bench and then put my head down, as Moslems do in praying, and I began to rock back and forth slowly because by doing that the thing that had taken possession of me, the sickness, the uselessness, whatever it was, seemed to go away. I half-slept, I half-prayed, and I thought, "What *is* this, for God's sake? What's the matter? Why is my head like a damned rock?"

At last I heard somebody at the door and quickly sat in the corner of the room, on the bench. My mother turned on a light, came in, and looked at me. I got up and fetched sawdust from the barn, so she could get the fire going, and in that way she wasn't able to notice that I was possessed, I was sick, I was useless, my head was a rock. Nobody would know.

The big event of 1958 was my son's sickness, known.

In 1957 I went from Malibu to New York to pick them up at the beginning of summer vacation, and took them to Venice by boat, and from there by train to Trieste, Belgrade, and Athens. And from there by boat to Naples and Barcelona, where we spent a month because the Avenida Hotel gave us a pleasant suite, and the food there was so good.

We decided to find out about Barcelona. Best for my son were the bullfights, to which he sometimes went alone. Best for my daughter were the *sardanas*, the public dancing of the Catalans.

And best for me was the two of them together.

In 1956 it was trips to New York, and drives from Malibu to San Francisco, Las Vegas, and Tijuana.

And that's far enough back for all practical purposes in this reverse chronology.

49   The Person

On a ship I once took, there was a boy with a guitar who liked to sing, "She rides the limousine, I buy the gasoline. Hot dog, that's where my money goes."

It was in February, snowing, and my son was not yet five months old. My daughter was two years from being born. I called her Lucy of course, after the old woman. I called my son Aram, because I would have wanted that name for myself had I had a choice. In my wallet I had a small snapshot of him and his mother, and I felt glad about them all the time. His mother was eighteen or nineteen, and I was thirty-five, the age my father had been when I was born.

Well, anything could happen now, because my son was there, the family line had been moved forward again, to another generation: and Petrus begat Armenak and Armenak begat William and William begat Aram, and so there was a chance that this might go on for some time to come.

Who begats who means something, if only the coming along of more names, each representing a new generation. As a kid I used to imagine that people a hundred years before 1918 must have been awfully incomplete. It never occurred to me that people even a thousand years ago, or possibly even ten thousand years ago, might very well have been the equal and possibly the superior of people in 1918, that they had the same individual differences, one from another, as people in 1918, and that on the whole, except for superficial changes of various kinds, the way of human life long ago was the same as it was in 1918. It may have been because I thought of them as a group, everybody together: the dead. Little by little, though, it came to me—so many things didn't come to me from books, even though I had done a great deal of reading, and so it had to take longer—that we were not the new thing I had always imagined we were. And we were not a new order of an old thing, either. We were the old thing itself. We were as good as *with* the great group I hadn't been for so long able to imagine as being formed of individuals, like my father and myself. Having come, we were as good as gone, like all of the previous generations. If you come, you've got to go, too. In the meantime, you just can't be said to be part of a great group, a mass, a collection of millions of individuals who are thereby rendered nameless, faceless, useless, and unremembered. For what had they done? They had begat. Their having begat had not been worthy of notice, but the fact remained that those they had begat were *there*, they were in the world, and so it was impossible not to notice *them*. There had been a long procession of the living-dying, and it promised to be just as long again, after which it might very well be just as long again, begat and begat and begat and begat, and by God there was my own begatting, there was the little snapshot of my son in the arms of his beautiful young mother.

I was looking at the snapshot when the boy with the guitar came along and asked to look at it, too. After he had done so, he showed me a snapshot of his daughter, who was a little beauty.

"Somebody told me you write books," he said. "Put me in a book some day, will you, in case I get killed, so my little girl will see her daddy in a book and be proud of him?"

"O.K."

"What'll you say about me?"

"I'll say, Johnny Clay played the guitar and sang, and I heard him."

Johnny was about twenty-five then, so now he's forty or forty-one, and his daughter, who was two then, is now eighteen, and her mother, who was about twenty-two then, she's thirty-eight. But if Johnny *was* killed, as he seemed to expect to be, he's not forty or forty-one, he's still twenty-five.

Some were killed and some weren't. The number killed was a big number but not nearly as big as the number not killed. Still, the number killed, if it included the guitar player, was one too many, for he was in no hurry at all, no guitar player is in a hurry, clarinet players are in a hurry. Banjo players are also in a hurry, also drummers.

An acquaintance in New York had one day said, "Nobody believes he'll be killed. Everybody believes somebody else may be, but he won't. I don't get it. I *know* I'm going to be killed." Well, he was a cut-up, and so I wanted to be straight-man for him, so he could come out with the punch-line.

"How are you going to be killed?"

"By cutting my finger on cellophane in opening a pack of cigarettes, that's how. I always get cut that way, and one of these days I'll get blood poisoning, or bleed to death."

Whoever was in *that* group and didn't want to be in it couldn't help thinking about getting killed, and how it might happen. *Anything* might do it, simply because a man was in the group and didn't want to be. Even something like being attacked and wounded by the tight cellophane around a pack of cigarettes might do it, as my acquaintance had put it, a critic and poet by profession, now a writer of lies on behalf of the cause. Having done well at it, having obeyed orders well, he was reasonably sure of a certain amount of security and a certain predictability about the future. If he chose, he could avoid being shipped simply by not insisting on it, but finally he *did* insist on it. I saw him in London, and he said, "Now, it's getting a little more dangerous, and I may get killed by a taxi."

Well, he wasn't, and neither was I, although I was driven mad, most likely, from three long, slow, endless years of dispossession and uselessness.

A year now is nothing, it is gone not before I know it but swiftly *while* I know it. It is not too swiftly gone, either, but differently gone. There is not so much new stuff in it as there had been in the years before the dispossession, not so much expectation. And so the dream moves along, the reality continues, the fantasy continues, and the remaining time grows less. Less and less, but only in terms of a long life, never in terms of a short one, for no man past fifty can imagine that he is not already ahead of the game, or that if he stops suddenly he is entitled to be astonished, for he has already had the best of it. He has been there not only twice but six or seven times.

Still, nothing is more to be desired (by the writer at any rate) than to go again, even if it is always the same, for it never actually is, because he himself is different every time, he is not who he was, he is not fifty-two any longer, he is going on fifty-three, and then he *is* fifty-three, and if his luck holds out, if the writing on his forehead, as old Lucy used to put it, *allows* it, if the writing there states that he *is* to stay, he *will* stay, he *shall* stay, he *shall have* stayed, for it was written that he would, that he should, that he shall have. I don't know what the writing upon my forehead may be, but if I have anything to do with it, being myself a writer, but unlike the Original Writer, unlike the Witness Himself, unlike the Teller of All, I shall write the writing on my own forehead, I shall *rewrite* what is written there, I shall revise it, improve it, give it better style, even if the writing comes to only one word, such as, for instance, Long, meaning a long life. And then in all probability I shall add two letters and make it Longer, and after enough more time has gone by, I shall revise the writing again and make it Longest.

50   The Purpose

In 1944, when I saw Shaw, he said he was dying, but he needn't have, for he was eighty-five. At eighty-five if you don't know you're dying, you don't know anything and can't learn.

He also said, quite simply, that he was senile. But when you know you're senile, you really aren't.

If I ever get to be eighty-five, and if I ever know I am senile, I will write a play about a man of eighty-five who knows he is senile.

As it is, I write plays now about men of fifty-two who are mad and know it.

And whether you're twenty-five, like Johnny Clay of Kentucky, or eighty-five, like Bernard Shaw of London by way of Dublin, you *know* you are dying.

Now, when Shaw told me he was dying, I didn't believe him, for he was too old to die. Only the young die, the old do something else. I won't say they go to sleep, because sleep is sleep precisely in that it is followed by waking.

A few days ago I finished a play called *Ho for Heaven* which is about the last sleep of a man who died. In the play I tried both to invent and to study one man's last sleep, his secret sleep, the sleep from which he did not waken. The man was a little older than fifty-two, he was fifty-seven, or so I *said,* at any rate. That man was not too old to die, but not quite old enough not to die, as Shaw didn't die.

Shaw ended it, that's what he did. The whole thing had acquired pretty good form, the line had moved here and there, making a form of some beauty and meaning, and then he stopped moving the line any longer, and the drawing, the life, the legend, and all the rest of it, were complete, and the one who had lived, the one who had drawn the picture, could be put with all the others who had had their fire but no longer had it.

"No, you're not dying at all," I said. "You will out-live us all."

And I didn't mean as a writer, by his works, which will in fact probably outlive most of the writing of the other writers, excepting of course my own, which no-body's writing will outlive. My writing will be dis-covered again and again. It will speak to the begatters and to the begotten as long as that business goes on, or as long as any writing speaks to anybody.

And when my writings stop speaking, if they ever do, then my drawings will start, and I have thousands of them.

51   The Water

During the summer of 1959 my kids and I, in the apartment on Avenue Victor Hugo, made a great many drawings.

We were tremendously alive there, fighting all the time, talking, disagreeing, shouting, being who we were, who we are. The paper my kids used was proper paper, bought at stores, but the only paper I wanted to use was the paper everybody else throws away: all kinds of wrapping paper, all kinds of throw-away leaflets that somebody in the street is always handing out, the paper inside empty cigarette packs, the unused sides of announcements, invitations, programs, score cards, letters, envelopes with my name, address and stamps on them.

My kids watched me put aside all such paper, and then they watched me put it to work.

I love paper, as I have remarked, and that means any kind of paper.

On scraps of all kinds I have put the first few words of many of my stories, novels, and plays, or the basic scheme, or method, or idea, or style of them. And I keep, I have always kept, these scraps.

Whenever I have come upon one, by accident, after ten years, or twenty, or longer, I have been astonished by the art of it, the power, the reality—the few quickly written words and the piece of useless paper itself, the envelope itself, or the announcement or invitation.

Time, and something more, has made the scrap of paper and the writing upon it a work of natural art, a people's art. Besides meaning what the written words mean, besides the connection of the words with a work I wrote, the scrap and the writing are a *picture,* and a deeply satisfying one, because the picture is so *unimportant,* swift, artless, and at the same time so right and true—because it *happened.*

I told my kids never to throw away anything they did in writing or drawing, at school or at home. I told them to put it away somewhere and forget it, because ten years later, or twenty, seeing it would please them, and they would learn a lot about themselves from it.

It may be that they heard me out, as kids do, but didn't see anything in the idea at all. Everybody goes his way as he chooses and must, and I am entirely willing to believe they throw away everything they do, and if that is so, I love them all the more for doing *that,* for love doesn't care about what's thrown away and what isn't, it cares only about the thrower, or the keeper.

Still, I will never be able to cherish those who throw away themselves and keep the money, because it just isn't a good transaction, it just isn't a fair exchange.

How could there possibly be anything more important for anybody to keep than himself? By which he in turn keeps in fact the whole human race, not just those he happens to know and love, or even those he happens to know and hate, but everybody.

One of the first things I wanted to have in this house out of storage was the drawings and paintings my kids and I did that summer, which they did not want. I had to have them, I had to see them, I had thrown away the money, but these were myself, and I wanted them in my house.

The drawings and paintings by my daughter are precisely herself, as if she had actually meant to make of them a self-portrait, and they are her as she was *then*, as she can never quite be again.

And that's how it is with the drawings of my son, too. I had to empty his waste-basket every day and smooth out the stuff he had thrown away, which he believed was no good, which I know was great, which I have and study all the time, seeing him, seeing his face and eyes and mouth and his whole being, inside and out, in every scrap he threw away, which I don't mind at all that he threw away, but which I must keep, since his worst, that which he believes to be his worst, is to me a treasure, for the day may come (my friend, for each of us) when he will not even bother to make something that he feels he needs to throw away because it isn't good enough, as good as it could be, the day may come when he will not even be interested in trying for anything at all in that arena, he may find his push from somebody unknown in my line or in his mother's line, and he may find that he only wants to push after the other stuff, and then these works of his childhood, boyhood, and young manhood will be (for me, at any rate) great works, thundering reminders of wealth lost, thrust aside in favor of abject unhealable poverty. And so it may be with my daughter, and if it must be so, then so let it be. I was against it, I hoped against it, I prayed against it, sitting with them in the great living room of that house, in the silence of concentration, of trying, each of us in that moment of trying immortal, unkillable, at the same time as fluid as water and as solid as rock.

Is this a father making too much of something, of very little, of so little as to be nothing? My friend, a father cannot make too much of anything related to his children, including the worst related to them, the worst in them. He can make mistakes of all kinds, he can hurt his kids when he believes he is helping them, he can offend them, he can shock them, even by who he is, even by the way he is who he is, and even by his love, but a father has got to make all he can of everything in and related to his kids, for until that is how it is, until sons find out how to become fathers, how to become both sons and fathers, the human race cannot have a father, it must go on having substitutes, and it has had them long enough.

And it isn't that God isn't a good substitute, and I mean *any* God, any *idea* of God. It is a grand substitute, it is great, it helps too many who would be without any father at all not to be great, or to be thrust aside. But having God is too easy an excuse for sons not to become fathers when it is time to become fathers, or at least to try, and to go on trying.

If a son begats a son, but does not become a father, he ceases even to be a son, he cannot be a son, and he moves away from, or even out of, the true human race, the race which believes at least that if there is no meaning, if there can be none, there can be a way of knowing, and of going, that (however senseless) is at least art, at least the equivalent of a scrap of paper with a few words on it, the back of a program with a drawing on it, at least an essay, an attempt, the evidence of having been there himself, aware of the worst but not also therefore unaware of the most, aware of the uselessness but not also therefore unaware of the usableness, open-eyed to all futility but not also therefore blind to the utility of love for its own simple sake, however flawed love may be, however charged with falsity, even.

Where is the father of the human race? He is in every son born, as the mother is in every daughter, and if the begatters of the sons and daughters begat and nothing else, or begat and be damned, begat and begone, how then shall the sons and daughters become the fathers and the mothers? And if every man is truly nobody's son and nobody's father, then where is the human race? Where is it to be found? Where is it to be known, fought, hated, and loved? And if the father and the mother do not make a home, how shall the human race make a home of the world? Shaw had no kids, but he may very well have been a father. He certainly was a father in his writing, but had he been a father in fact as well, who can guess how much more his writing might have been?

And it isn't necessary for a man's kids to be like him, or to think and feel as he thinks and feels, or to be better than he is, or greater. It is only necessary for a man's kids to be begotten, fathered, and mothered until they may in turn become first the fathers and mothers of their own fathers and mothers, and then the fathers and mothers of their own kids. A man is in fact born again in his son and in his daughter, and his son is his father and his daughter is his mother. And the more of them he has, the more sons and daughters, the more fathers and mothers, the more he himself may then enlarge his own sonhood and his own fatherhood. It cannot be done any other way. (And it isn't that I have spoken, as the joke goes, for in fact I have not, and as the Kid would have said, Not I, but the father. Of course they got it a little wrong, and he himself hurried himself out before he had had a chance to demonstrate what he really meant, which he might have done by in fact begatting, and then by becoming the father of which he had so frequently spoken, which *was* always himself, always in himself.)

We invent it all, we make it all, and if we don't, we don't, and so far not many of us have.

Does it matter if the river flowing to the sea doesn't understand the fish in it?

Nothing matters and nothing *needs* to matter, but if we are to make it, it is to be made, and *we* are to do it.

I wasn't a son to Shaw saying he was dying, and he wasn't a father to me. I haven't been a son to anybody except to my own father, unknown to me, except as he was revealed to me in myself. I have been a son only to the human race itself, which I now consider both my father and my son. And I won't pretend that this preoccupation is the consequence of my being a peasant. I am a worker, and at my best a hard worker who rejoices in his work, both disbelieving and believing in it. I am of the streets, of the towns and cities, and have in me much of their character, their mixture of aloofness and comradeship, their dignity and shabbiness, their indifference and care, and the hell with that, too. I am a peasant, too. The geometry of the vineyard is in me, the lore of the vine is mine, the growing of the grape is meaning to me, the eating of the grapes, and the drinking of the wine of them, is greatness in my lore, and the hell with that, too. I am a writer who writes, and the hell with that, too. I am a reader who reads, and the hell with that, too. I am the drawer of the drawings that fall one upon another like leaves from a great tree, and the hell with that, too. I am a man looking for a woman, for the one woman in the world who *is* my woman, one woman who *is* a woman, and glad to be, and the hell with that, too. I am a drinker who drinks three to any other drinker's one, but the hell with that, too. I am a braggart who brags about anything that is his, but the hell with that, too. I am a liar who tells the truth, the only truth, and in the same breath and in the same telling lies in his teeth, but the hell with that, too. I am a madman who is better balanced than any man who ever fell, who ever threw himself away from footing, or any man who did not fall and did not lose his footing, but the hell with that, too. I am Saroyan, but the hell with that, too.

There he goes, then. There goes you know who. *You*, my friend. Not me. I ain't going. I've got taxes to pay, and pieces to pick up.

The following fifteen pages of photographs have been purposely placed at the end of this book, rather than within the text itself, because they constitute a narrative of their own. For this reason they have been arranged chronologically and with a minimum of captions, most of them in the handwriting of the author.

The birthplace of my father and mother, and the home of the Saroyans until the turn of the century

Bitlis

Cosette   Takoohi   Zabel   Le Havre 1906
            Henris

Aram Saroyan   Lucy/Henry   Verkelne   Takoohi   Cosette   theHouse
Zabel

1906 X

(Upper) Erzeroum, 1906   (Lower) New York, 1907

Zabel   Takoohi   Henry   Armenak   Cosette   NY 1907

Mrs William Stonehill
Cosette

N.Y. 1908

Mihran Saroyan Armenak/WS   Takoohi Fresno 1910 X

Henry Saroyan   WS   San Jose 1911   +

Fresno 1915 Dikran Bagdasarian, Verkine Saroyan's husband ✗

Fresno 1915

Missak Saroyan, Armenak's brother

WS   George Jean Nathan
NY 1940

Sacramento 19## 1942   WS

WS   Atlantic 1944   X

WS   Paris 1945   Ross Bagdasarian X

San Francisco 1941   WS Lucy Garoghlanian Saroyan   X

Lucy Saroyan Aram Saroyan WS Tijuana mexico 1958 X

WS / Lucy / Aram Saroyan New York 1957 ✗

Armenian writers and W. S. in Erivan, Armenia, September 1960

Armenian poets, playwrights, and singer Badalyan

WS
1960 Erivan Armenia

Armenian actors, directors, and writers, Moscow, 1958

Cast of *Sam the Highest Jumper of Them All*, Theatre Royal, Stratford, London, April 1960